Cooking by Colour
for Health, Fitness and Energy

Cooking by Colour

for Health, Fitness and Energy

50 recipes shown step by step in over 300 photographs

CONTRIBUTING EDITOR: TRISH DAVIES

LORENZ BOOKS

This edition is published by Lorenz Books, an imprint of Anness Publishing Ltd
Hermes House, 88–89 Blackfriars Road, London SE1 8HA
tel. 020 7401 2077; fax 020 7633 9499

www.lorenzbooks.com; www.annesspublishing.com

If you like the images in this book and would like to investigate using them for
publishing, promotions or advertising, please visit our website
www.practicalpictures.com for more information.

UK agent: The Manning Partnership Ltd; tel. 01225 478444;
fax 01225 478440; sales@manning-partnership.co.uk

UK distributor: Book Trade Services; tel. 0116 2759086; fax 0116 2759090;
uksales@booktradeservices.com; exportsales@booktradeservices.com

North American agent/distributor: National Book Network;
tel. 301 459 3366; fax 301 429 5746; www.nbnbooks.com

Australian agent/distributor: Pan Macmillan Australia; tel. 1300 135 113;
fax 1300 135 103; customer.service@macmillan.com.au

New Zealand agent/distributor: David Bateman Ltd; tel. (09) 415 7664; fax (09) 415 8892

Publisher: Joanna Lorenz
Editor: Joy Wotton
Designer: Nigel Partridge
Jacket designer: Adelle Morris
Production controller: Christine Ni
Proofreading Manager: Lindsay Zamponi

ETHICAL TRADING POLICY
Because of our ongoing ecological investment programme, you, as our customer, can
have the pleasure and reassurance of knowing that a tree is being cultivated on your
behalf to naturally replace the materials used to make the book you are holding.
For further information about this scheme, go to www.annesspublishing.com/trees

© Anness Publishing Ltd 2010

A CIP catalogue record for this book is available from the British Library.

PUBLISHER'S NOTE
Although the advice and information in this book are believed to be accurate and true
at the time of going to press, neither the authors nor the publisher can accept any legal
responsibility or liability for any errors or omissions that may be made. The reader
should not regard the recommendations, ideas and techniques expressed and
described in this book as substitutes for the advice of a qualified medical
practitioner or other qualified professional. Any use to which the recommendations,
ideas and techniques are put is at the reader's sole discretion and risk.

Notes

Bracketed terms are intended for American readers.

For all recipes, quantities are given in both metric and imperial measures and,
where appropriate, in standard cups and spoons. Follow one set of measures,
but not a mixture, because they are not interchangeable.

Standard spoon and cup measures are level.
1 tsp = 5ml, 1 tbsp = 15ml, 1 cup = 250ml/8fl oz.

Australian standard tablespoons are 20ml. Australian readers should use 3 tsp in
place of 1 tbsp for measuring small quantities.

American pints are 16fl oz/2 cups. American readers should use 20fl oz/2.5 cups
in place of 1 pint when measuring liquids.

Electric oven temperatures in this book are for conventional ovens.
When using a fan oven, the temperature will probably need to be reduced by
about 10–20°C/20–40°F. Since ovens vary, you should check with your
manufacturer's instruction book for guidance.

The nutritional analysis given for each recipe is calculated per portion (i.e. serving
or item), unless otherwise stated. If the recipe gives a range, such as Serves 4–6,
then the nutritional analysis will be for the smaller portion size, i.e. 6 servings.

Measurements for sodium do not include salt added to taste.

Medium (US large) eggs are used unless otherwise stated.

**Main front cover image shows Peppers Filled with Spiced Vegetables
– for recipe, see page 46.**

Contents

Introduction

Brightly coloured food is not only a feast for the eye. By including more foods from each of the four major food groups – yellow and orange, red, green, and blue and purple – you can also improve the overall health and vitality of yourself, your friends and family. Each food group is valuable in fighting against particular kinds of illness and the traumas that can affect us all. Follow the rainbow diet as a part of your daily routine, always make sure that your shopping basket contains at least one item from each colour group, and find out how to lead a healthier life.

The Scientific Approach to Good Health

There is strong scientific evidence to show that eating a diet high in a variety of colourful cooked and raw vegetables and fruits can reduce the risk of several forms of cancer and arthritis, as well as keeping away such common ailments as eczema, recurrent colds, flu, asthma and bronchitis. If you suffer from any of these illnesses, it may mean

Below: Protect your body the natural way by shopping organically, following the rainbow diet and experimenting with a variety of many plant foods.

THOSE VITAL VITAMINS

Vitamins form an important part of our diet. This list explains their particular benefits as well as giving examples of the colours of the food most likely to contain them.

• **Vitamin A** is important for maintaining healthy skin. It helps prevent infections of the upper respiratory tract and improves night vision. It is found mainly in green and yellow/orange fruit and vegetables.

• **Vitamin B1** may increase concentration but it is destroyed by cooking or UV light. It is found in green vegetables.

• **Vitamin B2** guards against the effects of fatigue and depression. It is found in green vegetables.

• **Vitamin C** promotes tissue repair and wound healing and encourages the general health of the immune system. It is an antioxidant and plays an important role in the absorption of food. Try citrus fruits, including oranges and lemons, in the orange/yellow food group, salad leaves and broccoli in the green group, blueberries in the blue/purple group and all kinds of red fruits for healthy living.

• **Vitamin D** is essential for healthy bones and teeth. Sunlight is our main source of this vitamin. It is found in green foods such as spinach, Swiss chard and beet greens.

• **Vitamin E** is a powerful antioxidant helping to prevent degeneration of nerves and muscles in the body. It helps prevent cardiovascular disease. Yellow sweet potatoes are a good source of vitamin E.

• **Vitamin K** aids blood clotting and helps the body absorb calcium, thus guarding against osteoporosis. It is found in many green leafy vegetables.

that your immune system needs a boost. In addition, stress and depression can weaken your body's natural defences, so eating sensibly is extra important. Research has shown that a diet high in red fatty meats, processed meats, added salt, sugary foods, saturated fats and alcohol could encourage certain cancers to develop, so what we eat plays a large part in our welfare.

Colours on Your Plate

Creating a rainbow on your plate is a sensational way to get children and adults alike to experiment and try out new foods. Eating a balanced diet that includes a variety of plant food gives us a better chance of getting all the nutrients we need for optimum health.

Variety is essential if we are to get the best range of natural goodness from vegetables, fruits and other plant foods. Aim to eat as many different kinds as possible.

Before a shopping trip, try to plan your menus so that you are shopping wisely and choosing foods with a wide range of health-giving benefits. Focusing on the different colours is a good way to ensure that you include all the elements you need, especially if you choose vividly coloured foods such as

Above: Snacking on plenty of fresh fruit and vegetables will help children to grow up fit and healthy.

green nettles and curly kale, red beetroot (beet) and pomegranates, or purple blueberries. The recipes in this book will give you plenty of ideas for using them.

The Rainbow Diet

Variety in the diet is essential if you and those you care for are to get the best range of natural nutritional goodness from vegetables, fruits and plant foods.

WHAT ARE ANTIOXIDANTS?

Antioxidants is a term used to describe the groups of vitamins, minerals and phytochemicals found in foods, that help to protect the body from the damaging effects of oxygen-free radicals. These are unstable molecules that are created naturally by the body. They can also be produced by such toxins as tobacco, pollution and radiation from sunlight and radioactive materials. These toxins can be carcinogenic, meaning they can damage cells, leading to the development of cancer. Antioxidants are able to mop up free radicals or prevent them from forming, and it is thought that they could thereby help to prevent cell damage. Building more fruit and vegetables into your diet may guard against the risk of strokes.

Above: Adding many different-coloured ingredients to a chicken salad makes it as good to look at as it is healthy and delicious to eat.

The idea of creating a rainbow on your plate is certainly food for thought. By including more plant foods from each of the colour groups – yellow/orange, red, green and purple/blue – you will be ensuring that you're getting the best mix and blends of nutrients for healthy living every day.

Evidence linking food and nutrition to cancer risk is growing. Research into the precise nature of cancer has not yet clarified exactly what it is that turns a normal cell into a cancerous cell. Although we know that carcinogens such as chemicals, radiation, tobacco, asbestos and viruses can cause cancer, it is still not known precisely how or why. However it is becoming clear that nutritional, social, psychological and environmental factors also play a role in cancer, and that choosing foods from particular colour groups may help fight certain kinds of the disease.

Antioxidant nutrients, found in all yellow, red and orange fruits and vegetables, grains and seeds, can help quench excessive free radical production known to be associated with the development of many cancers.

It is not claimed that foods can cure cancer, but eating at least five or more portions of seasonal fresh fruit and vegetables a day certainly will help.

Inputting the rainbow diet into your everyday life and eating a rich variety of vegetables, fruits, nuts, pulses and legumes can play a large role in helping the body's systems.

Below: Green kiwi fruit, yellow bananas and purple grapes are all part of the rainbow diet as you include a mixture of brightly coloured foods in every meal.

The Rainbow Diet

A spectacular rainbow of colours of fresh vegetables and fruit is available today. We should all aim to eat a wide varied diet to ensure a good mix of vitamins and minerals. The rainbow diet is based on foods that can help you become energized and healthy.

Scientific studies have shown that the pigments that form the colour in fruit and vegetables are laden with phytochemical compounds and antioxidants, which strengthen the immune system and make the body stay fit, vitalized and healthy.

The colour of food affects our emotions and energy levels. Base your diet on all the colours of the rainbow, red, orange and yellow, green, and a mixture of blue, purple and indigo. Each colour affects our mood swings and feelings in a different way.

Try planning recipes or eating the right types of food to create a tailor-made plan to suit your feelings. It is important to balance different-coloured meals and ingredients each day, and this should provide you and your family with a healthy, well-balanced diet.

Below: Combine bright red berries, yellow and green melon, and sweet purple blueberries, passionfruit and borage flowers, to experience the rainbow diet.

The rainbow diet relates fruit and vegetable colours to the beneficial pigments in their flesh, roots, skin and leaves. This all-round diet helps you keep fit, gives a feeling of well-being and may protect you naturally from infections, chronic illness and disease. By eating a balanced diet that includes a variety of plant foods we stand a much better chance of getting all the nutrients we need for optimum health.

Follow the Rainbow

This rainbow diet depends on the different-coloured fruits and vegetables contained in each beneficial colouring (pigment). If we mix the different-coloured foods every day by eating at least five or more portions of fruit and vegetables, then we will benefit from the pigments in them.

Fresh fruit and vegetables are not the only foods we need, even when trying to lose weight. The rainbow diet is a long-term diet that helps you lose weight the natural way and stay healthy at the same time. It is a lifestyle change for all the family. The diet should also be rich in complex carbohydrates – such as washed and peeled potatoes, sweet potatoes, unrefined rice and wild rice, as well as a balanced source of protein – such as nuts, beans or animal foods including dairy products, meat, fish and shellfish.

Above: Freshly prepared salads will improve your children's well-being and vitality. Green leaves such as watercress are a natural antibiotic.

Discover the Super Foods

Food is a basic necessity that keeps us going all day and offers us many health benefits. Certain types of food such as fruits and vegetables, oily fish and other plant foods stand out of the nutritional crowd because they have special properties that make them unique in terms of how beneficial they can be to our health. Because of their

CRACK THE COLOUR CODE
The rainbow diet is based on the colours of the rainbow – red, orange and yellow, green, and purple and blue. Each of these colourful foods affects our moods differently. For example, recipes based mainly on red-coloured food are great when you feel tired and in need of a boost, but not so good if you are angry or need to relax. If you eat meals based on a specific colour according to how you feel, you can create your own designed meal plan to suit you. It is important to get a balance of different-coloured meals each day.

Above: Pears, fruit juice, peppers, tomatoes and leafy vegetables are rich in vitamin C, stimulate the digestive system and are powerful cleansers.

health-enhancing qualities these foods are sometimes referred to as super foods. The nutrients contained within these foods can assist with many of the body's natural functions such as digestion, boosting the immune system, strengthening bones and helping to protect against various forms of cancer.

The Hidden Benefits of Super Foods

The list below is just a selection of the foods that have been shown to be particularly valuable for health, but research always continues. These superfoods are believed to help boost the body's immune system, thus keeping it more resistant to illnesse and disease.

Aronia Berries are full of antioxidants, which help protect against heart disease and cancer. They are high in vitamins B and C and are a good source of folic acid.

Bananas are a perfect food – high in nutrients containing potassium, zinc, iron, folic acid, calcium, vitamin B and fibre. Good for digestion and helpful in cases of sickness or diarrhoea.

Brazil Nuts are rich in the mineral selenium, which has antioxidant effects that may help protect against cancer.

Selenium can also help to keep the immune system strong. Be careful of taking selenium supplements as a high dose can be toxic.

Garlic is known as the king of healing plants. Scientists have proved that it reduces cholesterol, lowers blood pressure, helps stops blood clotting and improves the circulation. Garlic is good for chest infections. It has also been shown to have antibacterial, antifungal, antiviral and anti-cancer properties.

Green Tea helps protect against heart disease, cancer, tooth decay, arthritis and bone loss. Green tea is high in flavonoids, which are thought to help cancer prevention.

Red, Yellow & Orange (Bell) Peppers are a great source of vitamin C. Just half a pepper will provide you with your daily requirement. They are also a useful source of flavonoids and betacarotene, which might help to oppose the free radical damage that can lead to cancer.

Salmon is an oily fish and a perfect source of Omega 3 fats. Best known for their beneficial effects on the heart, these fats may also help to prevent cancer and enhance the immune system. Salmon is also a good source of selenium. Try to eat oily fish at least twice a week.

Turmeric is a ground dried root, which is a rich source of iron, calcium, vitamin B and magnesium and aids immunity by enhancing the health of the liver. It also cleans up free radicals and so helps fight degenerative diseases. It may also help to prevent the formation of cancer cells.

Virgin Olive Oil contains phenolic antioxidants, which give it a greeny tinge. It is a monounsaturated fat, which means it is good oil as it does not raise blood cholesterol. Virgin olive oil is rich in Vitamin E but, like all oils, it is high in calories.

Below: A dried fruit compote is a healthy and versatile standby. Pitted prunes, apricots and raisins are rich in fibre and antioxidants.

How to Eat by Colour

Choose your meals from each of the four main colour groups – orange/yellow, red, green and blue/purple – for a diet that will leave you feeling relaxed, stress-free and bursting with energy. It is essential to drink plenty of water, as well as vitamin-rich juices and herbal teas. Try to cut down on stimulants such as tea, coffee and alcohol, which may induce the production of free radicals. Choose foods from a particular colour group if there is a particular area in your life that you wish to address, or mix and match the colours to get the full benefit of the rainbow diet.

It is now accepted that food may play a vital part in the prevention and development of some cancers. Phytoestrogens found in soya, seeds and other vegetables may help to regulate oestrogen dominance – one of the contributing factors in hormone-related cancers. Antioxidants found in all red, orange and yellow fruits and vegetables, fish, grains and seeds can quench excessive free radical production known to be associated with the development of many cancers.

Colours play an important part in our life, from what we wear to what we eat. Our mood swings are affected by colour. If you feel like relaxing, choose purple food. If you want or need a boost of energy, focus on red food. For an instant and often effective antidepressant, try yellow and orange foods such as oranges or peaches.

A Diet of Many Colours

These menus may help to boost the immune system and combat diseases on a daily basis. Begin every day with breakfast to get you off to a healthy start. Taking time out for lunch will restore your natural energy levels and give you stamina. The evening meal is a time to relax and an important time to maintain good health. Ensure that your diet is rich in antioxidant nutrients – vitamins A, C, and E and such minerals as zinc and selenium – by choosing foods across the whole colour spectrum.

The Sunshine Menu
Orange and yellow foods contain many powerful antioxidants such as vitamin C and bioflavonoids. They are thought to bring joy and happiness, stimulate the brain and act as antidepressants.

Breakfast
• Mango Mania
• Sliced bananas with yogurt

Lunch
• Date, Orange and Carrot Salad
• Baked Peaches

Evening Meal
• Carrot and Coriander Soup
• Glazed Sweet Potatoes with Bacon
• Grilled Mango Cheeks with Lime Syrup and Sorbet

The Red-hot Menu
For a day filled with energy choose your meals from the red foods. Their red pigment contains lycopene. Red foods can improve vision at night, strengthen the heart and boost the immune system.

Breakfast
• Red Defender
• Griddled Tomatoes on Soda Bread

Lunch
• Apple and Beetroot Salad with Red Leaves
• Strawberries with Passion Fruit

Evening Meal
• Tomato and Fresh Basil Soup
• Red Pepper Risotto
• Raspberry Fromage Frais and Amaretti Scrunch

The Great Green Menu

Going green with a diet rich in leafy vegetables, green grapes, apples and limes can improve vision, maintain strong bones and teeth and fight against cancer. Cook green food very briefly to avoid destroying vitamins.

Breakfast
- Wheatgrass Tonic
- Green grapes and pears or other fresh green fruit

Lunch
- Spinach and Roast Garlic Salad
- Baked Stuffed Apples

Evening Meal
- Mixed Green Leaf and Herb Salad
- Persian Omelette
- Ginger and Kiwi Sorbet

The Healing Blues Menu

Blue and purple foods are a way of helping you relax and gain peace of mind. They are often high in vitamin E, which may prevent wrinkles, and vitamins A and C to aid eye disorders and improve circulation.

Breakfast
- Cool as a Currant
- Fresh blueberries and blackberries

Lunch
- Sweet and Sour Red Cabbage
- Fresh Figs Baked with Honey, Vanilla and Cinnamon

Evening Meal
- Aubergine Soup with Mozzarella and Gremolata
- Duck with Plum Sauce
- Blackcurrant Water Ice

The Rainbow Diet

For a magnificent and nutritionally balanced day choose your foods from all the colour groups – orange and yellow, red, green, and blue and purple – combining them to ensure you get all the nutrients you need.

Breakfast
- Minted Pomegranate Yogurt with Grapefruit Salad

Lunch
- Chilled Stuffed Courgettes
- Rose Water-scented Oranges with Pistachio Nuts

Evening Meal
- Carrot and Coriander Soup
- Peppers filled with Spiced Vegetables
- Damson Water Ice

yellow and orange

THE SUNSHINE COLOURS

These fruits and vegetables have a wonderful range of colours from pale yellow to rich burnt orange. Carrots, squashes, pumpkins, mangoes, pineapples and citrus fruits are all powerful yellow and orange plant foods. Most of these fruits and vegetables are super-rich in betacarotene, which is converted into the immune-boosting antioxidant vitamin A. They may help protect the body from certain types of cancer, reduce intestinal inflammation and help detoxify the body.

What yellow & orange foods to eat

These coloured foods are thought to bring joy and happiness and to improve intellect. Orange and yellow foods may also stimulate the brain and act as a powerful antidepressant.

Eating orange- and yellow-coloured food may help give you a healthy heart, improve vision, especially at night, and also boost the immune system. In some cases, it may also help lower the risk of some cancers.

Yellow Vegetables

Carrots contain large amounts of carotene and vitamin A, along with useful amounts of vitamins B3, C and E. When eaten raw, they also provide good quantities of potassium, calcium, iron and zinc, but these benefits are reduced when carrots are boiled.

Corn is a good source of vitamins A, B and C. Its antioxidant properties are increased when cooked, helping to fight cancer and heart disease and protect against cataracts.

Pumpkins are large, bright yellow or orange squashes, which contain a deep orange flesh. They are rich in

Below: Corn on the cob and baby corn

betacarotene which helps to reduce certain types of cancer and lowers the risk of heart disease. Pumpkin seeds may help to reduce the risk of prostate cancer.

Squashes, including butternut, acorn and other varieties, are rich in betacarotene, which supports the immune system, aids wound healing and promotes healthy skin.

Swedes (Rutabagas) are a good source of calcium, for healthy bones and teeth, and potassium, which may play a role in decreasing blood pressure.

Turmeric is a yellow spice that acts as a natural antiseptic and antibacterial agent. It is often used as a natural treatment for arthritis and rheumatoid arthritis.

Yellow and Orange (Bell) Peppers are high in antioxidant carotenoids and orange peppers contain zeaxanthin, a compound known to protect against cataracts and macular degeneration.

Yellow Beets are an excellent provider of potassium. The leaves, which have the flavour of spinach, are high in vitamin A, iron and calcium.

Yellow Courgettes (Zucchini) are a member of the same family as the somewhat straighter green courgettes. Yellow courgettes have a slightly firmer flesh, and they supply useful amounts of potassium and folic acid, which is essential in the production of healthy red blood cells and to prevent anaemia.

Yellow Tomatoes, like other varieties of tomatoes, are high in vitamin A, vitamin C, calcium, potassium and lycopene, which may help in the prevention of heart disease and cancer. They can improve skin texture and colour and are also a good way of purifying the blood.

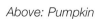

Above: Pumpkin

Left: Tomatoes

Yellow Fruits

Apricots, both the dried and the fresh, contain the antioxidant betacarotene, and are a rich source of iron and other minerals and vitamin A.

Bananas are extremely nutritious, being rich in potassium, riboflavin, niacin and dietary fibre. They also contain vitamins A and C and some calcium and iron. They are thought excellent for low-salt, low-fat and cholesterol-free diets.

Cantaloupe Melons may aid the body in its fight against cancer and macular degeneration. The more orange the flesh of a cantaloupe melon, the more beneficial carotenes it contains.

Fresh and Ground Ginger can guard against motion sickness and vomiting. Ginger tea is recommended by many researchers as a guard against migraine and arthritis pain.

Golden Kiwi Fruit were developed by New Zealand growers in the late 1970s. They have an edible skin and like green kiwi fruit are very rich in vitamin C.

Grapefruit are a good source of dietary fibre and vitamin C; one fruit will provide 1.5 times the adult daily requirement of vitamin C. Eat them in moderation since they may encourage cancer growth.

Above and right: Oranges, lemon and grapefruit

Honeydew Melons have a very high water content, making them very low in calories. Look for orange flesh honeydew melons, which contain more beneficial carotenes.

Lemons are rich in vitamin C, which builds up the immune system, and they are very low in calories. They contain flavonoid, a compound that is rich in antioxidant and anti-cancer properties.

Mangoes, when ripe, are rich in vitamins, especially A and C. They are a good source of betacarotene, a natural compound that may improve eyesight, especially night vision, and promote a healthy heart.

Nectarines are a good source of potassium and phosphorus, dietary fibre and vitamins A and C.

THE SUNSHINE FOODS

Yellow and orange foods are widely known as 'sunshine' foods. They are a rich source of antioxidants, and many people think they may provide a protective action against many types of cancer.

Turmeric
Carrots
Peaches
Mangoes
Apricots
Corn
Macadamia and Brazil nuts
Sunflower seeds
Yellow (bell) peppers
Linseed oil
Saffron

Oranges and the Citrus Family, including tangerines, easy peelers etc., are an excellent source of vitamin C, which promotes tissue repair and wound healing and improves the general health of the immune system. It is an antioxidant and plays an important role in the absorption of iron and the formation of antibodies.

Papayas are rich in vitamin A and calcium, and contain large quantities of the enzyme papain, which breaks down protein and can be used to tenderize meat. Papain also makes this fruit very easy to digest.

Peaches are a good source of vitamin A, which helps prevent infections of the upper respiratory tract, vitamin B, which can fight fatigue and depression, and vitamin C.

Persimmons (Sharon Fruit) are rich in vitamin A. They yield potassium, calcium and iron. Persimmons contain phenolic compounds, which are claimed to help fight athero-sclerosis, a leading cause of heart disease, heart attacks and strokes.

Physalis (Cape Gooseberry) are fully ripe when the fruit has a bright golden colour. They are packed with Vitamin C and will help the body defend itself naturally against colds and other respiratory illnesses.

Pineapples are rich in both vitamin C and dietary fibre. They contain bromelain, an enzyme that aids digestion, so are the perfect fruit to finish a rich meal. Pineapples are rich in manganese, a mineral which helps the body build healthy bones.

Yellow Apples, like other apples, are high in pectin and are a good source of soluble and insoluble fibre, which may promote a healthy heart and maintain regularity. They contain small amounts of potassium, which may aid general health and help maintain healthy blood pressure.

Yellow/Golden Raspberries are a valuable source of vitamin C, potassium, niacin and riboflavin, and dietary fibre.

Yellow Pears contain a small amount of vitamins A and C as well as some potassium and riboflavin. Potassium can act as a tonic for anyone who is recovering from illness or an operation, and riboflavin plays a key role in energy metabolism.

Yellow Watermelons, like red and pink watermelons, have a high water content and are low in calories. They contain some vitamins B and C.

Below: Pears

Health benefits of yellow & orange foods

The photo pigment of yellow and orange fruits and vegetables is given by betacarotene, a natural compound found in pumpkins, butternut squash, saffron and carrots. All these fruits and vegetables have a differing amount of vitamins A and K. These colourful foods support the immune system, aid wound healing and promote healthy skin. The fruits and vegetables are a good source of valuable powerful antioxidants such as vitamin C, as well as carotenoids and bioflavonoids, two classes of phytochemicals that scientists are studying for their health-promoting potential. They may help to protect the body against lung and other types of cancer.

Yellow- and orange-coloured fruits and vegetables can also be useful in treating chronic viral infections such as herpes simplex. The properties of yellow and orange foods may help prevent the formation of cancer cells and can protect against heart disease, stomach ulcers, poor eye sight and arthritis. They play a role in regulating blood sugar levels.

Below: Oranges are full of vitamin C.

Above: Pineapple

The Colour of Detachment, Happiness and Joy

Choose foods from this group at times of the day when you're nervous, need to concentrate or make decisions but not when you are stressed. If you feel lacking in energy, orange and yellow food certainly can give you a boost.

The Benefits of Betacarotene

The orange/yellow pigment is given by the betacarotene, a natural compound that improves eyesight, especially night vision, and helps the body keep a healthy heart. It is thought to strengthen the immune system, prevent against cancer, particularly of the bowel, and is a great anti-ageing and anti-wrinkling agent for the skin.

Above: Carrots

Betacarotene is a pigment that is usually related and connected to vitamin A-rich foods such as carrots, mangoes and papayas. It is also found in pumpkins, sweet potato, saffron, turmeric, oranges and other orange-coloured citrus fruit, bananas, mangoes and pears. Betacarotene is stored under the epidermis, which is a layer of skin cells in the subcutaneous fatty

ACTIVATE THE ANTIOXIDANTS
Antioxidants are thought to protect the body from certain types of cancer and are useful in treating a wide range of ailments from poor eyesight to stomach ulcers. The yellow and orange fruits and vegetables support the liver and kidneys, making them an excellent aid to detoxification, and they also have antiviral properties, which boost protection against infection. Eat plenty of these sunshine foods every week as part of your low-fat healthy diet.

Above: Peaches and nectarines

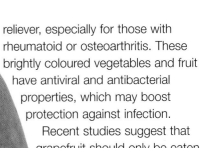

Above: Mango

tissue. It has a very important function as the super-rich betacarotene absorbs ultra-violet rays without allowing them to damage the tissues of the skin. This is how the natural protection of the skin works against the harmful effects of the sun. Carotene can be stored in the liver and then, when the body needs it, it is converted into vitamin A.

The carotenes in some fruit and vegetables gives them their vivid orange and yellow colour. Carrots and pumpkins contain alphacarotene, which some studies suggest helps against cervical and other cancers. They may also support liver and kidney functions, making them good for detoxification.

Below: Butternut squash

Other Benefits

Oranges, lemons, squash and other yellow and orange fruits and vegetables contain varying quantities of such antioxidants as vitamin C and powerful bioflavonoids. Fruits such as fresh pineapple and yellow kiwi fruit contain a protein-digesting enzyme (bromelain), which mimics the action of pancreatic enzymes and may reduce inflammation and swelling and thus be a good pain reliever, especially for those with rheumatoid or osteoarthritis. These brightly coloured vegetables and fruit have antiviral and antibacterial properties, which may boost protection against infection.

Recent studies suggest that grapefruit should only be eaten in moderation because they may encourage cancer growth.

These antioxidants may also protect the body from certain types of cancer and are useful in treating a range of ailments from poor eye sight to stomach ulcers. The yellow and orange fruits and vegetables support the liver and kidneys, making them an excellent source of detoxification, and they also contain antiviral properties, which boost protection against infection. Eat one or more portions of these sunshine foods every day as part of your low-fat diet.

Below: Melons are low in calories and high in betacarotenes, helping you become slimmer and fitter.

Apricot squash

Apricots promote detoxification and help extract waste from the body. They can also have a balancing effect on the nervous system. Fresh and dried apricots will stabilize blood sugar levels and are rich in vitamins A and B, calcium, iron, magnesium and zinc. They are a good antioxidant detoxifying agent and are beneficial for pregnant and elderly people.

1 Squeeze the limes and oranges, either by hand or using a citrus juicer. Halve and stone (pit) the apricots.

2 Put the apricots in a blender or food processor with a little of the citrus juice and the lemon balm, and blend until smooth, scraping the mixture down from the side of the bowl, if necessary. Add the remaining juice and blend until completely smooth.

3 Pour into chilled medium glasses and serve decorated with extra lemon balm.

Makes 2 glasses

2 limes
3 oranges
4 ripe apricots
several sprigs of lemon balm, plus extra
    to decorate

Cook's tip
This makes a tangy, invigorating blend to wake up your senses. Stir in a little clear honey or sugar to sweeten if you find it too tart.

Energy 46kcal/195kJ; Protein 0.9g; Carbohydrate 10.9g, of which sugars 10.9g; Fat 0.2g, of which saturates 0g; Cholesterol 0mg; Calcium 17mg; Fibre 1.1g; Sodium 9mg.

Mango mania

This is a delicious zesty, dairy-free, low-fat drink that stimulates the immune system and may also help protect mucous membranes from pathogens. Mango contains an enzyme papin, which helps to digest proteins. These fruits are rich in vitamins, natural sugar, fibre and anti-allergic, antibacterial, anti-cancer antioxidants.

Makes 2 tall glasses

1 medium mango
300ml/½ pint/1¼ cups soya milk
finely grated rind and juice of 1 lime,
    plus extra rind for garnish
15–30ml/1–2 tbsp clear honey
crushed ice

1 Using a sharp knife, peel the mango and cut the flesh off the stone (pit). Place the chopped flesh in a blender or food processor and add the soya milk, lime rind and juice and a little honey. Blend until smooth and frothy.

2 Taste the mixture and add more honey, if you like, blending until well mixed. Place some crushed ice in two glasses, then pour over the smoothie. Sprinkle with lime rind and serve.

Cook's tip
For a very sweet drink, use soya milk sweetened with apple juice.

Energy 111kcal/468kJ; Protein 4.9g; Carbohydrate 17.1g, of which sugars 16.9g; Fat 2.6g, of which saturates 0.6g; Cholesterol 0mg; Calcium 29mg; Fibre 2g; Sodium 51mg.

Pumpkin soup with rice

Pumpkins are a good source of vitamin A, carotenoids and antioxidants and are low in calories. They are thought to help to prevent the formation of cancer cells and may also promote healthy skin. Pumpkin seeds can be roasted and added to salads where they form a good source of fatty acids, phosphorus, zinc and magnesium.

Serves 4

Ingredients
1.1kg/2lb 7oz pumpkin
750ml/1¼ pints/3 cups
   chicken stock
750ml/1¼ pints/3 cups semi-skimmed
   (low-fat) milk
10–15ml/2–3 tsp sugar
75g/3oz/½ cup cooked white rice
salt and ground black pepper
5ml/1 tsp ground cinnamon,
   to garnish

1 Cut the pumpkin into slices. Remove and discard the seeds from the pumpkin, cut off the peel and chop the flesh.

2 Place in a pan and add the stock, milk, sugar and seasoning. Bring to the boil, then reduce the heat and simmer for about 20 minutes, or until the pumpkin is tender. Drain the pumpkin, reserving the liquid, and purée it in a food processor, then return it to the pan with the liquid.

3 Bring the soup back to the boil, add the rice and simmer for a few minutes until it is heated through. Pour into bowls and dust with cinnamon.

Energy 202kcal/856kJ; Protein 9.7g; Carbohydrate 33.1g, of which sugars 15.6g; Fat 4.4g, of which saturates 2.5g; Cholesterol 11mg; Calcium 315mg; Fibre 2.8g; Sodium 82mg.

Carrot and coriander soup

Carrots are super-rich in betacarotene, which the body converts into the immune-boosting antioxidant vitamin A. Carrots may support the liver and kidney function, making them excellent for detoxification. These bright-coloured vegetables are also thought to have antiviral and antibacterial properties, boosting your protection against infection.

Serves 4

450g/1lb carrots, preferably young
  and tender
15ml/1 tbsp sunflower oil
40g/1½oz/3 tbsp butter
1 onion, chopped
1 stick celery, plus 2–3 pale leafy tops
2 small potatoes, peeled
900ml/1½ pints/3¾ cups boiling
  vegetable stock
10ml/2 tsp ground coriander
15ml/1 tbsp chopped fresh coriander (cilantro)
150ml/¼ pint/⅔ cup milk
salt and ground black pepper

1 Trim and peel the carrots and cut them into even chunks. Heat the oil and 25g/1oz/2 tbsp of the butter in a large pan and fry the onion over a gentle heat for 3–4 minutes or until slightly softened. Do not let it brown.

2 Slice the celery sticks and chop the potatoes coarsely, and add to the onion in the pan. Cook for 2 minutes, then add the carrots and cook for 1 minute.

3 Pour the boiling vegetable stock over the vegetables, then season with salt and ground black pepper. Cover the pan with the lid and simmer for 30 minutes or until the vegetables are tender.

4 Reserve 6–8 tiny celery leaves from the leafy tops for the garnish, then finely chop the remaining celery tops. Melt the remaining butter in a large pan and add the ground coriander. Fry for about 1 minute, stirring constantly, until the aromas are released.

5 Reduce the heat under the pan and add the chopped celery tops and fresh coriander. Fry for about 30 seconds, then remove the pan from the heat.

6 Ladle the soup into a food processor or blender and process until smooth, then pour into the pan with the celery tops and fresh coriander. Stir in the milk and heat gently until the soup is piping hot. Check the seasoning, then serve in warmed bowls garnished with the reserved celery leaves.

Energy 168kcal/697kJ; Protein 3g; Carbohydrate 11.9g, of which sugars 9.2g; Fat 12.4g, of which saturates 6g; Cholesterol 24mg; Calcium 94mg; Fibre 3.1g; Sodium 758mg.

Moroccan carrot salad

This root dish is made from tender freshly cooked carrots. Carrots appear to support the immune system, aid wound healing and promote healthy skin. They are rich in vitamin A and K, folate, calcium, iron, zinc and carotenoids and fibre. They may help prevent the formation of cancer cells and can also protect the body against heart disease and arthritis.

Serves 2

3–4 carrots, thinly sliced
1.5ml/¼ tsp ground cumin, or to taste
60ml/4 tbsp garlic-flavoured oil and
    vinegar dressing
30ml/2 tbsp chopped fresh coriander (cilantro)
    leaves or a mixture of coriander and parsley
salt and ground black pepper

Variation
Replace the cumin with 15ml/1tbsp toasted sesame seeds, a useful source of calcium and vitamin E.

1 Cook the thinly sliced carrots by either steaming or boiling in lightly salted water until they are just tender but not soft. Drain the carrots, leave for a few minutes to dry and cool, then put into a mixing bowl.

2 Add the ground cumin, garlic dressing and herbs. Season to taste and chill well before serving. Check the seasoning just before serving and add more ground cumin, salt or black pepper, if required.

Energy 53kcal/220kJ; Protein 0.6g; Carbohydrate 4.2g, of which sugars 3.9g; Fat 3.9g, of which saturates 0.6g; Cholesterol 0mg; Calcium 29mg; Fibre 1.6g; Sodium 15mg.

Date, orange and carrot salad

A delicious combination of detoxifying fruit and vegetables. Raw crunchy carrots are one of the effective detoxifiers helping the liver and kidneys. Carrots are rich in antioxidants and may protect the body from certain types of cancer; they boost the immune system and can prove useful in treating and alleviating a range of ailments from poor night vision to stomach ulcers.

Serves 4

1 Little Gem (Bibb) lettuce
2 carrots, finely grated
2 oranges
115g/4oz fresh dates, stoned (pitted) and cut into eighths, lengthways
25g/1oz/¼ cup toasted shelled whole almonds, chopped
30ml/2 tbsp lemon juice
15ml/1 tbsp orange flower water

Variation
Substitute another citrus fruit, such as pink grapefruit or clementines.

1 Separate the lettuce leaves, wash and pat them dry, then arrange the leaves in a salad bowl or on individual serving plates.

2 Place the grated carrot in a mound on top of the lettuce.

3 Peel the oranges and cut them into segments. Arrange them around the mound of grated carrot. Pile the dates on top, then sprinkle with the toasted almonds. Mix together the lemon juice and orange flower water and sprinkle over the salad. Serve the salad chilled.

Energy 138kcal/582kJ; Protein 3.6g; Carbohydrate 21.8g, of which sugars 21.4g; Fat 4.7g, of which saturates 0.4g; Cholesterol 0mg; Calcium 90mg; Fibre 3.9g; Sodium 18mg.

Stuffed baby squash

Squashes come in a variety of different shapes and sizes but have lots of things in common, being a good source of vitamins A and E, rich in carotenoids and antioxidants, as well as having anti-cancer properties. They help aid normal blood cell function and encourage healthy muscles and nerves. Squashes are a good natural laxative and play a part in a healthy diet.

Serves 4

4 small squash, each about 350g/12oz
200g/7oz/1 cup mixed wild and basmati rice
60ml/4 tbsp chilli and garlic oil
150g/5oz/1¼ cups grated Gruyère cheese
salt

1 Preheat the oven to 190°C/375°F/ Gas 5. Pierce the squash several times. Bake for 30 minutes or until tender.

2 Cook the rice in salted, boiling water for 12 minutes, and then drain.

3 Leave the squash until they are cool enough to handle. Slice a lid off the top of each squash, discard the seeds, and scoop out and chop the flesh.

4 Heat the oil in a frying pan and cook the chopped squash for 5 minutes. Reserve 60ml/4 tbsp of the cheese, and add the remainder to the pan with the rice and a little salt. Mix well.

5 Pile the mixture into the squash shells and place in an ovenproof dish. Sprinkle with the remaining cheese and bake for 20 minutes.

Cook's Tip
This recipe works well with acorn squash and butternut squash, which are rich in both betacarotene and vitamin E, antioxidants that are believed to promote health and reduce the risk of certain cancers.

Energy 483kcal/2011kJ; Protein 15.9g; Carbohydrate 48.2g, of which sugars 6.4g; Fat 24.3g, of which saturates 10.1g; Cholesterol 36mg; Calcium 396mg; Fibre 3.8g; Sodium 271mg.

Pumpkin, rosemary and chilli risotto

Pumpkin and butternut squash are thought to help prevent the formation of cancer cells, heart disease and mental dysfunction, and to promote healthy skin. These vegetables help the blood cells function well and encourage healthy muscles and nerves within the body. Fresh rosemary is claimed to be a traditional tonic for the heart as well as calming on the digestive system.

Serves 4

115g/4oz/½ cup butter

1 small onion, finely chopped

2 large garlic cloves, crushed

250g/9oz fresh pumpkin or butternut squash, peeled and roughly chopped

1 fresh red chilli, seeded and finely chopped

30ml/2 tbsp chopped fresh rosemary

250g/9oz/1½ cups risotto rice, preferably Arborio or Vialone Nano

about 750ml/1¼ pints/3 cups hot chicken stock, preferably fresh

50g/2oz/⅔ cup freshly grated Parmesan cheese, plus extra to serve

salt and ground black pepper

1 Melt half the butter in a heavy pan, add the onion and garlic, and cook for 10 minutes. Add the pumpkin or squash and chilli and cook, stirring constantly, for 5 minutes. Stir in the rosemary.

2 Add the rice, and stir with a wooden spoon. Cook for 2–3 minutes to toast the rice grains without browning.

3 Begin to add the stock, a ladleful at a time, stirring all the time until each ladleful is absorbed into the rice. The rice should always be bubbling slowly. If not, add some more stock.

4 Continue adding the stock until the rice is tender and creamy but the grains remain firm and the pumpkin is beginning to disintegrate. (This should take about 20 minutes, depending on the type of rice used.) Taste and season well with salt and pepper.

5 Stir the remaining butter and the Parmesan cheese into the rice. Cover and let the risotto rest for 2–3 minutes, then serve straightaway with extra Parmesan cheese.

Energy 506kcal/2102kJ; Protein 10.3g; Carbohydrate 52.4g, of which sugars 1.9g; Fat 28.1g, of which saturates 18.2g; Cholesterol 79mg; Calcium 188mg; Fibre 0.8g; Sodium 352mg.

Sweet potato, pumpkin and prawn cakes

Look out for the yellow sweet potato as this has a higher amount of vitamins A and B and contains carotenoids, which may boost the immune system and protect against viral infections. Sweet potatoes help boost energy levels since they have a low glycaemic index, so that energy is released gradually over time. This vegetable is an extremely good antioxidant and antiviral.

Serves 4

200g/7oz/1⅔ cups strong white bread flour
2.5ml/½ tsp salt
2.5ml/½ tsp dried yeast
175ml/6fl oz/¾ cup warm water
1 egg, beaten
200g/7oz fresh prawn (shrimp) tails, peeled
225g/8oz pumpkin, peeled, seeded
   and grated
150g/5oz sweet potato, grated
2 spring onions (scallions), chopped
50g/2oz water chestnuts, chopped
2.5ml/½ tsp chilli sauce
1 garlic clove, crushed
juice of ½ lime
vegetable oil, for frying
lime wedges, to serve

1 Sift together the flour and salt into a large bowl and make a well in the centre. In a separate container, dissolve the yeast in the water until creamy then pour into the centre of the flour and salt mixture. Pour in the egg and set aside for a few minutes until bubbles appear. Mix to form a smooth batter.

2 Place the prawns in a pan with enough water to cover. Bring to the boil, then reduce the heat and simmer for 10 minutes. Drain, rinse in cold water and drain again. Chop, then place in a bowl with the pumpkin and sweet potato.

3 Add the spring onions, water chestnuts, chilli sauce, garlic and lime juice and mix well. Fold into the batter mixture carefully until evenly mixed.

4 Heat a 1cm/½in layer of oil in a large frying pan until really hot. Spoon in the batter in heaps, leaving space between each one, and fry until golden on both sides. Drain on kitchen paper and serve with the lime wedges.

Energy 317kcal/1346kJ; Protein 18.2g; Carbohydrate 57.6g, of which sugars 9.1g; Fat 3.2g, of which saturates 0.9g; Cholesterol 145mg; Calcium 216mg; Fibre 6g; Sodium 383mg.

Glazed sweet potatoes with bacon

Sweet potatoes are easy to digest and score low on the glycaemic index. Their distinctive colour betacarotene is converted into vitamin A, which as an antioxidant helps to reduce intestinal inflammation. The sweet taste of the glazed potatoes complements the bacon flavour in this recipe. The cooking process also aids the body to absorb more carotenoids.

Serves 4–6

butter, for greasing
900g/2lb sweet potatoes
115g/4oz/½ cup soft light brown sugar
45ml/3 tbsp butter
30ml/2 tbsp lemon juice
4 rashers (strips) smoked lean bacon, cut
    into matchsticks
15ml/1tbsp chopped fresh parsley
salt and ground black pepper

1 Preheat the oven to 190°C/375°F/ Gas 5 and lightly butter a shallow ovenproof dish. Cut each unpeeled sweet potato crosswise into three and cook in boiling water, covered, for about 25 minutes or until just tender.

2 Drain and leave to cool. When cool enough to handle, peel and slice thickly. Arrange in a single layer, overlapping the slices, in the prepared dish.

3 Sprinkle the sugar over the sweet potatoes and dot the dish evenly with small pieces of butter.

4 Sprinkle over the lemon juice, top with bacon and season well. Bake for 35–40 minutes, basting once or twice.

5 The sweet potatoes are ready once they are tender, test them with a knife to make sure. Remove from the oven once they are cooked.

6 Preheat the grill (broiler) to a high heat. Sprinkle the sweet potatoes with chopped parsley.

7 Place the ovenproof dish under the grill for 2–3 minutes until the sweet potatoes are browned and the bacon is crispy. Serve hot.

Energy 387kcal/1627kJ; Protein 7.2g; Carbohydrate 49.5g, of which sugars 26.1g; Fat 19.3g, of which saturates 9.8g; Cholesterol 50mg; Calcium 49mg; Fibre 3.6g; Sodium 562mg.

Grilled mango cheeks with lime syrup and sorbet

Mangoes are bursting with antioxidants thanks to their high vitamin C content. The rich orange-coloured flesh also contains vitamin E, carotenoids, phosphorus, carotenes and natural sugar. Mango is thought to have an astringent effect on the gut, which means that it may promote contractions and encourage digestive processes.

Serves 6

250g/9oz/1¼ cups sugar
juice of 6 limes
3 star anise
6 small or 3 medium to large mangoes
groundnut (peanut) oil, for brushing

1 Place 250ml/8fl oz/1 cup water in a heavy pan and add the sugar. Heat gently until the sugar has dissolved. Increase the heat and boil for 5 minutes. Cool and add the lime juice and any pulp that has collected in the squeezer. Strain and reserve 200ml/7fl oz/scant 1 cup in a bowl with the star anise.

2 Pour the remaining liquid into a measuring jug or cup and make up to 600ml/1 pint/2½ cups with cold water. Pour into a freezerproof container. Freeze for 1½ hours, stir well and return to the freezer for another hour until set.

3 Transfer the sorbet mixture to a processor and pulse to a smooth icy purée. Freeze for another hour or longer, if wished. Alternatively, make the sorbet in an ice cream maker; it will take about 20 minutes, and should then be frozen for at least 30 minutes before serving.

4 Pour the reserved syrup into a pan and boil for 2–3 minutes, or until thickened a little. Leave to cool. Cut the cheeks from either side of the stone (pit) on each unpeeled mango, and score the flesh on each in a diamond pattern. Brush with a little oil. Heat a griddle, until very hot. Lower the heat a little and grill the mango halves, cut-side down, for 30–60 seconds until branded with golden grill marks.

5 Invert the mango cheeks on individual plates and serve hot or cold with the syrup drizzled over and a scoop or two of lime sorbet. Decorate with the reserved star anise.

Cook's tip
If this dessert is part of a larger barbecue meal, cook the mangoes in advance using a griddle set over the first red hot coals. Set aside until ready, and serve cold.

Energy 63kcal/272kJ; Protein 2g; Carbohydrate 14.5g, of which sugars 14.3g; Fat 0.2g, of which saturates 0.1g; Cholesterol 0mg; Calcium 12mg; Fibre 2g; Sodium 32mg.

Pineapple and mango with vanilla

Pineapple and mango are tropical fruits laden with enzymes such as bromelain (which is used in various medicines including anti-inflammatory drugs). They aid digestion and reduce inflammation, helping to break down the proteins as well as lowering blood pressure and relieving angina.

Serves 4

1 large pineapple
1 large mango
25g/1oz/2 tbsp unsalted butter, melted
4 thick slices panettone or brioche

For the vanilla yogurt
250g/9oz/generous 1 cup Greek (US strained
 plain) yogurt
30ml/2 tbsp clear honey
2.5ml/½ tsp ground cinnamon
a few drops natural vanilla extract, to taste

1 To prepare the pineapple, cut the bottom and the spiky top off the fruit. Stand the pineapple upright and cut off the skin using a sharp knife, removing all the spikes, but as little of the flesh as possible. Discard any brown sections of the flesh.

2 Lay the pineapple on its side and cut the fruit into quarters. Peel and discard the skin. Remove and discard the core if it is hard. Cut the pineapple into thick wedges.

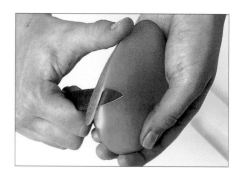

3 To prepare the mango, cut away the two thick sides of the mango as close to the stone (pit) as possible. Peel the mango, then cut the remaining flesh from the stone. Slice the fruit and discard the stone.

4 Heat a griddle pan over a medium heat. Add the pineapple and mango to the pan (you may need to do this in batches if your pan is small). Brush the pineapple and mango with melted butter, and cook for 8 minutes, turning once, until soft and slightly golden. Alternatively, heat the grill (broiler) to high and line the rack with foil. Place the pineapple and mango on the foil, brush with butter and grill (broil) for 4 minutes on each side.

5 Meanwhile, place the yogurt in a bowl with the honey, cinnamon and vanilla and stir well.

6 Lightly toast the panettone or brioche, then serve on warmed plates, topped with the pineapple and mango and accompanied by the vanilla yogurt.

Energy 411kcal/1736kJ; Protein 9.9g; Carbohydrate 64.1g, of which sugars 42g; Fat 15.4g, of which saturates 7.7g; Cholesterol 14mg; Calcium 202mg; Fibre 4.7g; Sodium 278mg.

Baked peaches

Peaches are a diuretic and laxative. They are a good source of vitamins A, B and C, and of copper, magnesium, phosphorus, zinc and natural sugar. Peaches can also aid the digestive system in that they can help prevent bladder stones.

Serves 4

4 ripe peaches
45ml/3 tbsp fresh apple juice
45ml/3 tbsp clear honey
10ml/2 tsp almond extract
low-fat probiotic yogurt, to serve

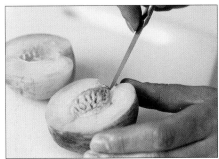

Cook's tips
• You can cook these peaches over a barbecue. Place them on sheets of foil, drizzle over the fruit juice mixture, then scrunch the foil around them to seal. Cook for 15–20 minutes.
• For a special occasion, you could use Amaretto di Sarone liqueur in place of the apple juice.

1 Preheat the oven to 190°C/375°F/ Gas 5. Cut each of the peaches in half and twist each of the two halves in opposite directions to separate them. Once you have separated the two halves, prise out the stones (pits) with the point of the knife.

2 Place the peaches cut side up in a roasting pan.

3 In a small bowl, mix the apple juice with the honey and almond extract, and drizzle over the halved peaches, covering them evenly.

4 Bake the peaches for 20–25 minutes, or until tender. Place two peach halves on each serving plate and drizzle with the pan juices. Serve immediately, with low-fat probiotic yogurt.

Energy 70kcal/299kJ; Protein 1.1g; Carbohydrate 17.3g, of which sugars 17.3g; Fat 0.1g, of which saturates 0g; Cholesterol 0mg; Calcium 8mg; Fibre 1.5g; Sodium 3mg.

Oaty pancakes with caramel bananas and pecan nuts

Firm ripe yellow bananas are a good source of energy and easy to digest, making them ideal as a quick breakfast for young and old. They contain vitamins A, B and C, zinc, folic acid and potassium, which is essential for the functioning of all cells in our bodies. They are useful in the management of gastro-intestinal disorders and also help to prevent high blood pressure.

3 Heat a large, heavy-based, lightly oiled frying pan. Using about 30ml/2 tbsp of batter for each pancake, cook 2 or 3 pancakes at a time. Cook for 3 minutes on each side or until golden. Keep warm while you cook the remaining 7 or 8 pancakes.

4 To make the caramel bananas and pecan nuts, wipe out the frying pan and add the butter. Heat gently until the butter melts, then add the maple syrup and stir well. Add the bananas and pecan nuts to the pan.

5 Cook the bananas and pecan nuts for about 4 minutes, turning once, or until the bananas have just softened and the sauce has caramelized. Take care not to burn the maple syrup.

6 To serve, place two pancakes on each of five warm plates and top with the caramel bananas and pecan nuts. Serve immediately.

Serves 5

75g/3oz/⅔ cup plain (all-purpose) flour
50g/2oz/½ cup wholemeal (whole-wheat) flour
50g/2oz/½ cup porridge oats
5ml/1 tsp baking powder
pinch of salt
25g/1oz/2 tbsp golden caster (superfine) sugar
1 egg, beaten
15ml/1 tbsp sunflower oil, plus extra
    for frying
250ml/8fl oz/1 cup semi-skimmed (low-fat) milk

For the caramel bananas and pecan nuts
50g/2oz/4 tbsp butter
15ml/1 tbsp maple syrup
3 bananas, peeled, halved and
    quartered lengthways
25g/1oz/¼ cup shelled pecan nuts

1 To make the pancakes, mix together the flours, oats, baking powder, salt and sugar in a bowl.

2 Make a well in the centre of the flour mixture and add the egg, oil and a quarter of the milk. Mix well, then gradually add the rest of the milk. Leave to rest for 20 minutes in the refrigerator.

Energy 394kcal/1652kJ; Protein 8.1g; Carbohydrate 49.5g, of which sugars 23.2g; Fat 19.5g, of which saturates 7g; Cholesterol 62mg; Calcium 108mg; Fibre 2.9g; Sodium 109mg.

Rose water-scented oranges with pistachio nuts

Oranges are high in vitamin C, a powerful antioxidant and anti-inflammatory agent. This brightly coloured fruit is also a good source of fibre and folic acid. They stimulate the immune system, liver function and appetite. Oranges may also help to lower levels of cholesterol in the blood. Eating whole oranges counts towards your portions of fruit and vegetables each day.

Serves 4

4 large oranges
30ml/2 tbsp rose water
30ml/2 tbsp unsalted shelled pistachio nuts,
  roughly chopped

Cook's tip
Rose-scented sugar is delicious lightly sprinkled over fresh fruit salads. To make, wash and dry a handful of rose petals and place them in a sealed container filled with caster (superfine) sugar for 2–3 days. Remove the petals before using the sugar.

1 Slice the top and bottom off one of the oranges to expose the flesh. Using a small serrated knife, slice down between the pith and the flesh, working around the orange, to remove all the peel and pith. Slice the orange into six rounds, reserving any juice. Repeat with the remaining oranges.

2 Arrange the orange rounds on a serving dish. Mix the reserved juice with the rose water and drizzle over the oranges. Cover the dish with clear film (plastic wrap) and chill for about 30 minutes. Sprinkle the chopped pistachio nuts over the oranges just before serving.

Energy 91kcal/384kJ; Protein 2.7g; Carbohydrate 11.3g, of which sugars 11.1g; Fat 4.3g, of which saturates 0.6g; Cholesterol 0mg; Calcium 67mg; Fibre 2.6g; Sodium 46mg.

red

THE COLOUR OF ENERGY

For a day filled with vitality and get up and go, choose your meals from the red food groups. This colour of food is bursting with energy and action. Choose this colour to boost your resources and help you change direction. If your favourite colour is red you are generally very ambitious, direct and sometimes impulsive, and always try to be the best at everything.

Specific phytochemicals in this red group have been studied for their health-promoting properties, including anthocyanins and lycopene. Red fruit and vegetables can help build a healthy heart and aid memory function.

What red foods to eat

Red-coloured fruits and vegetables will help you feel energetic and on top of the world. They contain varying amounts of all kinds of valuable powerful antioxidants such as vitamin C, carotenoids and bioflavonoids.

Recipes that are based mainly on red foods are good when you feel tired and require an extra boost of energy to get you through the day. Eating this type of coloured food can help maintain a healthy heart, and may improve vision especially at night, and boost the immune system. Red-coloured food may also help to lower the risk of some cancers within the body.

Red Vegetables

Beetroot (Beet), whether raw or cooked, is an excellent provider of potassium for a healthy heart. The leaves have the flavour of spinach and are high in vitamin A, iron and calcium.

Kidney Beans are red in colour and are a very good source of cholesterol-lowering fibre.

Radicchio is a good source of vitamins C, E and K, folate, potassium, copper and manganese. Its characteristic red colour indicates the presence of anthocyanins, vegetable pigments, which may act as antioxidants.

Radishes are rich in vitamin C, which is an antioxidant and plays a important role in the absorption of iron and the formation of antibodies. Radish greens contain far more vitamin C, calcium and protein than the red roots.

Red (Bell) Peppers are packed with beta-carotene, which is converted to vitamin A by the body and is essential for night vision.

Red Chillies are high in vitamin A, a potent antioxidant and boost to the immune system. The capsaicin (the chemical that gives chillies their hot taste) stimulates the digestive process. Chillies are said to lower blood cholesterol, and thus benefit both the heart and blood vessels.

Red Lentils are a great source of iron for the vegetarian, which helps to fortify the blood. Lentils are high in dietary fibre, which helps relieve constipation and lowers blood cholesterol.

Red Onions contain vitamins B and C together with calcium, iron and potassium. They contain cycloallin, an anticoagulant, which helps protect against heart disease.

Red Potatoes are a very good source of vitamin C, and during the winter potatoes were once the main source of this vitamin. They also contain potassium, iron and vitamin B.

Tomatoes contain a red pigment known as lycopene, which appears to act as an antioxidant, neutralizing the free radicals that can damage cells in the body, and may inhibit the development of stomach, lung and breast cancers. They are high in vitamin A, vitamin C, potassium and iron.

Above: Tomatoes

Left: Radishes

Red Fruits

Blood Oranges are rich in antioxidants, including vitamin C, which aids healing, boosts the immune system and helps in the absorption of iron. The characteristic blood red colour indicates that it contains anthocyanins, which fight AIDS-related illnesses, and flavons, which reduce inflammation.

Cherries contain vitamins A and C and dietary fibre. They have powerful antioxidants called anthocyanins,

RED FOR ENERGY
All these red ingredients are rich in vitamins, minerals and have diuretic qualities. They stimulate the immune system and help to fight off infection. They can also reduce inflammation of the digestive tract and bacterial activity in the bowel.

Strawberries
Watermelons
Red (bell) peppers
Redcurrants
Tomatoes
Radishes
Red potatoes
Cranberries
Pomegranates
Raspberries

Right: Red potatoes

Above: Beetroots

which may lower cholesterol, reduce inflammation and help maintain a healthy heart. The red compounds may also help those with arthritis and gout.

Cranberries are a super berry, containing vitamins C and D, potassium and iron. They were considered to be a good protection against scurvy.

Below: Strawberries

Pink and Red Grapefruit are an excellent source of dietary fibre and vitamin C. Their rich red and pink colouring shows that they contain lycopene, a phytonutrient, which fights against cancer.

Pomegranates are rich in vitamin C and are a good source of dietary fibre.

Raspberries are a valuable source of vitamin C, potassium, niacin and riboflavin, and dietary fibre. Raspberry juice is said to be good for the heart, while raspberry leaf tea is said to help prevent miscarriages, ease labour and help the uterus to contract after the birth of a child.

Red Apples contain small amounts of vitamins C and A. They are high in pectin and a good source of dietary fibre. Red apples are rich in anthocyanins, which give plants their red colour and have been shown to boost health through their antioxidant activity.

Red Grapes are highly nutritious, containing natural sugars, potassium, iron and dietary fibre. Their rich red colour demonstrates that they are a source of flavonoids, which might help to oppose the free radical sun damage that can eventually lead to cancer.

Red Pears contain a small amount of vitamins A and C and some potassium and riboflavin. They are rich in lycopene, which may help prevent certain types of cancer including prostate cancer.

Redcurrants are high in vitamin C, manganese and potassium. They contain anthocyanins, which may help protect cells from oxidative damage.

Rhubarb contains significant amounts of calcium, potassium and thiamine and has natural laxative properties.

Strawberries are rich in vitamins B and C and contain considerable amounts of potassium, iron and fibre. They contain anthocyanins, which make them red and are antioxidants that are efficiently absorbed into the body.

Above: Raspberries and redcurrants

Watermelons are high in water content and hence they are low in calories. They contain vitamins B and C. They also contain lycopene, a red pigment that is an excellent antioxidant that can help prevent heart disease and some forms of cancer.

Below: Cranberries

Health benefits of red foods

The red pigment in many fruits and vegetables contains health-promoting substances such as lycopene (antioxidant carotenoids), vitamins A and C and anthocyanins (antioxidants). Generally they help to improve the immune system response while also helping to maintain energy levels. This combination makes these foods a useful addition to the diet of those suffering from energy compromising conditions such as cancer and AIDS. They boost resistance to infectious disease, encouraging wound healing and keeping the skin and mucous membranes in good condition.

It is further claimed that these fruits and vegetables may protect against cancer. They may aid in maintaining normal blood fat levels and the production of haemoglobin by the red blood cells.

Eat these foods to ensure that you are getting the best mix of nutrients for healthy living every day. A good piece of advice is to make sure the foods you

Below: Strawberries are not only delicious but are rich in anthocyanins, a great source of antioxidants.

Above: Watermelon

and your family eat are not refined, and check to see if they contain any hidden salt and sugar. Dried fruit snacks, based on preserved cherries, cranberries or strawberries, may appear healthy, but they can contain a lot of added sugar.

Red foods are thought to encourage a healthy nervous system, and they may protect you against asthma, depression and migraine.

The Colour of Energy

Choose foods from this red group at times of the day when you feel tired or mellow, but not if you are angry or want to relax. All these red ingredients are rich in vitamins, minerals and have diuretic qualities. They stimulate the immune system and help to fight off infection. They can reduce inflammation of the digestive tract and bacterial activity in the bowel.

There are all kinds of simple ways to include more fruit and vegetables in your diet. Begin the day with a fresh fruit for breakfast and add fruit or vegetables to your main meals. Snack on cherry tomatoes and semi-dried or fresh strawberries, raspberries and cranberries instead of crisps and biscuits. Have a bowl of fresh fruit on display for everyone to eat instead of sweets and biscuits.

Eat seasonally. Let blood oranges, red apples and pears see you through winter. Enjoy sun-warmed strawberries and raspberries in the height of summer. Look out for tomatoes, red grapes and pomegranates as late season fruit ripens.

Below: Raspberries

EAT TO LIVE
Eating a well-balanced healthy diet, packed with fruit and vegetables, is really important as it can help to prevent illness in the future. It is never too late for you to live a healthier life. Start by making sensible dietary choices every day, such as eating and drinking plenty of the freshest seasonal fruits and vegetables available and other plant foods such as herbs. Summer red fruits such as watermelon and cherries can help maintain a healthy heart and urinary tract, and may even aid memory function. Serve them simply as an amazing natural remedy that will prevent and treat illness and guard against disease.

Right: Tomatoes

Above: Strawberries, cherry tomatoes and other hand-held fruit make a wonderfully healthy snack for children.

Lycopene for Health

The red pigment contains the lycopene antioxidant, from the carotenoids family of pigments, which helps our memory, protects and helps prevent some forms of cancer and heart problems, helps maintain optimum health and promotes iron absorption. It is thought to be extremely beneficial against cancer of the prostate and testicles as well as cervical and breast cancer.

Besides the antioxidant properties, lycopene is also a detoxifier of the waste in the body, and it inhibits cholesterol formation.

Lycopene is present in the red fruits, including strawberries, raspberries, redcurrants and watermelons and also in such vegetables as red (bell) peppers, tomatoes and red onions.

Left: Pomegranates

Other Benefits

Many red fruits are also a great source of vitamin C. Beetroot is a valuable source of iron and helps to fortify the blood. It has a concentrated source of vitamins and minerals, particularly folic acid and potassium, which can act as a tonic for any one who is recovering from Illness or operations.

Tomatoes are a good source of lycopene and claimed to be especially beneficial for men to protect against prostate cancer. Generally, it is best to eat raw fruits and vegetables but by cooking tomatoes it releases higher levels of lycopene. It may reduce the effect of prostate cancer by as much as 40–45 per cent.

Below: Red pepper and radish

Red defender

Red berries are packed full of immune boosters, such as bioflavonoids and pro-anthocyanins, and rich in vitamin C. Strawberries are a tonic, laxative and antibacterial, and may help the gall bladder and liver functions. Watermelon and grapes are a powerful mixture of antioxidants with vitamins A, C and B3 that may inhibit the action of allergies, viruses and carcinogens.

Makes 2 glasses

200g/7oz/1¾ cups strawberries
90g/3½oz red grapes, seeded
1 small wedge of watermelon

1 Hull the strawberries and halve if large, reserving two for decoration. Skin the watermelon, reserving two chunks for decoration.

2 Put the watermelon in a blender or food processor and blend until the seeds are broken up. Add the strawberries and grapes and blend until completely smooth, scraping the mixture down from the side of the bowl. Serve in tall glasses, decorated with the reserved fruit.

Cook's tip
Everyone is encouraged to eat more fruit and vegetables. If you want to build extra fruit into your diet, serve this juice with chunks of watermelon or strawberry halves.

Energy 85kcal/362kJ; Protein 1.5g; Carbohydrate 20.1g, of which sugars 20.1g; Fat 0.5g, of which saturates 0.1g; Cholesterol 0mg; Calcium 29mg; Fibre 1.5g; Sodium 9mg.

Cherry berry trio

This smoothie consisting of cherries, strawberries and grapes is rich in vitamins A, B and C, iron, magnesium, natural sugar and bioflavonoids. It is reputed that it may help cleanse and purify the digestive system, cleanse the blood and aid elimination of waste products throughout the body, making this drink a great way to start the day.

Makes 2 large glasses

200g/7oz/1¾ cups strawberries
250g/9oz/2¼ cups red grapes
150g/5oz/1¼ cups red cherries, pitted
ice cubes

1 Halve two or three strawberries and grapes and set aside with a few perfect cherries for decoration. Cut up any large strawberries, then push them through a juicer with the remaining grapes and cherries.

2 Pour into glasses, top with the halved fruits, cherries and ice cubes, and serve immediately. To make a fun decoration, skewer a halved strawberry or grape on a cocktail stick (toothpick) and hang a cherry by its stem.

Cook's tip
The cherry season passes all too swiftly, so enjoy them to the full in this refreshing blend of red juices.

Energy 138kcal/587kJ; Protein 2g; Carbohydrate 33.9g, of which sugars 33.9g; Fat 0.3g, of which saturates 0g; Cholesterol 0mg; Calcium 42mg; Fibre 2.7g; Sodium 10mg.

Pepper soup with Parmesan toast

Red and yellow peppers boost immunity, helping protect against cancer. They are rich in antioxidants, vitamins A, B and C, carotenoids and fibre. They also help maintain normal blood-fat levels, thus helping the production of haemoglobin in the blood cells. It is believed peppers encourage a healthy nervous system. Tomatoes contribute lycopene and extra fibre.

Serves 4

1 onion, quartered
4 garlic cloves, unpeeled
2 red (bell) peppers, seeded and quartered
2 yellow (bell) peppers, seeded and quartered
30–45ml/2–3 tbsp olive oil
grated rind and juice of 1 orange
200g/7oz can chopped tomatoes
600ml/1 pint/2½ cups cold water
salt and ground black pepper
30ml/2 tbsp chopped fresh chives,
   to garnish (optional)

For the hot Parmesan toast
1 medium baguette
50g/2oz/¼ cup butter
175g/6oz Parmesan cheese

1 Preheat the oven to 200°C/400°F/ Gas 6. Put the onion, garlic and peppers in a roasting pan. Drizzle the oil over the vegetables and mix well, then turn the pieces of pepper skin sides up. Roast for 25–30 minutes, until slightly charred, then allow the vegetables to cool slightly.

2 Squeeze the garlic flesh out of the skins into a food processor or blender. Add the roasted vegetables, orange rind and juice, tomatoes and water. Process until smooth.

3 Press the mixture through a sieve (strainer) into a bowl. Season well and chill for 30 minutes.

4 Make the Parmesan toasts when you are ready to serve the soup. Preheat the grill (broiler) to high. Tear the baguette in half lengthways, then tear or cut it across to give four large pieces. Spread the pieces of bread with butter.

5 Pare most of the Parmesan into thin slices or shavings using a swivel-bladed vegetable knife or a small paring knife, then finely grate the remainder.

6 Arrange the sliced Parmesan on the toasts, then dredge with the grated cheese. Transfer the cheese-topped baguette pieces to a large baking sheet or grill (broiler) rack and toast under the grill for a few minutes until the topping is well browned.

7 Ladle the chilled soup into large, shallow bowls and sprinkle with chopped fresh chives, if using, and plenty of freshly ground black pepper.

8 Serve the browned hot Parmesan toast with the chilled soup.

Energy 124kcal/516kJ; Protein 2.4g; Carbohydrate 15g, of which sugars 14.2g; Fat 6.4g, of which saturates 1g; Cholesterol 0mg; Calcium 23mg; Fibre 3.5g; Sodium 13mg.

Tomato and fresh basil soup

Tomatoes are rich in betacarotene and lycopene, another antioxidant from the carotene group, which helps to protect eye tissues. They are also rich in vitamins A, B and C, folic acid and fibre. Recently research has shown that they may help to combat prostate cancer and reduce inflammation of the digestive tract and bacterial activity in the bowel.

Serves 4

15ml/1 tbsp olive oil
25g/1oz/2 tbsp butter
1 onion, finely chopped
900g/2lb ripe tomatoes, roughly chopped
1 garlic clove, roughly chopped
about 600ml/1 pint/2½ cups
   vegetable stock
120ml/4fl oz/½ cup dry white wine
30ml/2 tbsp sun-dried tomato paste
30ml/2 tbsp shredded fresh basil
150ml/¼ pint/⅔ cup double (heavy) cream
salt and ground black pepper
whole basil leaves, to garnish

1 Heat the oil and butter in a large pan until foaming.

2 Add the finely chopped onion and cook gently for about 5 minutes, stirring, until the onion is softened but not brown, then add the chopped tomatoes and garlic.

3 Add the stock, white wine and sun-dried tomato paste to the pan and stir to combine. Heat until just below boiling point, then carefully pour the mixture into the ceramic cooking pot of a slow cooker.

4 Switch the slow cooker to the high or auto setting, cover with the lid and cook for 1 hour. Leave the slow cooker on auto or switch to low and cook for a further 4–6 hours, until tender.

5 Leave the soup to cool for a few minutes, then ladle into a food processor or blender and process until smooth. Press the puréed soup through a sieve (strainer) into a clean pan.

6 Add the shredded fresh basil and the cream to the soup and heat through, stirring. Do not allow the soup to reach boiling point. Check the consistency and add a little more stock if necessary. Season, then pour into warmed bowls and garnish with basil. Serve immediately.

Cook's tip
If you cannot obtain fresh basil leaves, then substitute frozen or dried basil in the soup.

Energy 335kcal/1387kJ; Protein 3.1g; Carbohydrate 11.7g, of which sugars 10.8g; Fat 28.9g, of which saturates 16.4g; Cholesterol 65mg; Calcium 50mg; Fibre 3g; Sodium 168mg.

Griddled tomatoes on soda bread

Red tomatoes are rich in the antioxidant lycopene, even if eaten cooked, canned, puréed or sun-dried. Tomatoes have been claimed to reduce the risk of heart disease, cancer (particularly prostate cancer) and appendicitis and are a good source of vitamins, flavonoids and potassium, which can help regulate blood pressure.

Serves 4

olive oil, for brushing and drizzling
6 tomatoes, thickly sliced
4 thick slices soda bread
balsamic vinegar, for drizzling
salt and freshly ground black pepper
shavings of Parmesan cheese,
   to serve

Cook's tip
Using a griddle pan reduces the amount of oil required for cooking the tomatoes and gives them a barbecued flavour.

1 Brush a griddle pan with olive oil and heat. Add the tomato slices and cook for about 4 minutes, turning once, until soft and slightly blackened. Alternatively, heat a grill (broiler) to high and line the rack with foil. Grill (broil) the tomato slices for 4–6 minutes, turning once.

2 Meanwhile, lightly toast the soda bread. Place the tomatoes on top of the toast and drizzle each portion with a little olive oil and vinegar.

3 Season to taste and serve immediately with thin shavings of Parmesan.

Energy 172kcal/724kJ; Protein 3.9g; Carbohydrate 25.1g, of which sugars 5.8g; Fat 6.9g, of which saturates 0.9g; Cholesterol 0mg; Calcium 63mg; Fibre 2.3g; Sodium 171mg.

Red pepper risotto

The combination of red peppers and tomatoes make this an ideal dish rich in vitamin C. It is also a useful source of flavonoids and betacarotene, both of which might help to oppose the free radical sun damage that can eventually lead to cancer. Red peppers also boost the immune system and help to maintain normal blood sugar and fat levels.

Serves 6

3 large red (bell) peppers
30ml/2 tbsp olive oil
3 large garlic cloves, thinly sliced
1½ x 400g/14oz cans chopped tomatoes
2 bay leaves
1.2–1.5 litres/2–2½ pints/5–6¼ cups
    vegetable stock
450g/1lb/2½ cups arborio rice (Italian risotto
    rice) or brown rice
6 fresh basil leaves, snipped
sea salt and ground black pepper

1 Preheat the grill (broiler). Put the peppers in a grill pan and grill (broil) until the skins are blackened and blistered all over. Put them in a bowl, cover with several layers of damp kitchen paper and leave for 10 minutes. Peel off the skins and slice the peppers, discarding the core and seeds.

2 Heat the olive oil in a wide, shallow pan. Add the garlic and tomatoes and cook over a gentle heat for 5 minutes, then add the pepper slices and bay leaves. Stir well and cook for 15 minutes more.

3 Pour the vegetable stock into a pan and heat it to simmering point. Stir the rice into the vegetable mixture and cook for 2 minutes, then add two or three ladlefuls of the hot stock. Cook, stirring occasionally, until the stock has been absorbed.

4 Continue to add stock in this way, making sure each addition has been absorbed before pouring in the next. When the rice is tender, season with salt and pepper to taste. Remove the pan from the heat, cover and leave to stand for 10 minutes before stirring in the basil and serving.

Energy 501kcal/2099kJ; Protein 10.9g; Carbohydrate 103.8g, of which sugars 13.6g; Fat 4.4g, of which saturates 0.7g; Cholesterol 0mg; Calcium 44mg; Fibre 3.9g; Sodium 20mg.

Peppers filled with spiced vegetables

Red and yellow peppers are rich in betacarotene and other antioxidants, which help keep a healthy heart and reduce blood cholesterol. This dish is packed full of flavour with lots of AIDS-immunity spices such as turmeric, helping to mop up free radicals.

Serves 6

6 large evenly shaped red or yellow
  (bell) peppers
500g/1¼lb waxy potatoes
1 small onion, chopped
4–5 garlic cloves, chopped
5cm/2in piece fresh root ginger, chopped
1–2 fresh green chillies, seeded and chopped
105ml/7 tbsp water
90–105ml/6–7 tbsp groundnut (peanut) oil
1 aubergine (eggplant), cut into 1cm/½in dice
10ml/2 tsp cumin seeds
5ml/1 tsp kalonji seeds
2.5ml/½ tsp ground turmeric
5ml/1 tsp ground coriander
5ml/1 tsp ground toasted cumin seeds
pinch of cayenne pepper
about 30ml/2 tbsp lemon juice
salt and ground black pepper
30ml/2 tbsp chopped fresh coriander
  (cilantro), to garnish

1 Cut the tops off the red or yellow peppers, then remove and discard the seeds. Cut a thin slice off the base of the peppers, if necessary, to make them stand upright.

2 Bring a large pan of lightly salted water to the boil. Add the peppers and cook for 5–6 minutes. Drain and leave the peppers upside down in a colander.

3 Bring a large pan of salted water to the boil. Cook the waxy potatoes for 10–12 minutes, until just tender.

4 Remove the potato pan from the heat. Drain the potatoes, then cool and peel them, and cut the potatoes into 1cm/½in dice.

5 Put the onion, garlic, ginger and green chillies in a food processor or blender with 60ml/4 tbsp of the water and process to a purée.

6 Heat 45ml/3 tbsp of the oil in a large, deep frying pan and cook the aubergine, stirring occasionally, until browned on all sides. Remove from the pan and set aside. Add another 30ml/ 2 tbsp of the oil to the pan and cook the potatoes until lightly browned. Remove from the pan and set aside.

7 If necessary, add another 15ml/ 1 tbsp oil to the pan, then add the cumin and kalonji seeds. Fry briefly until the seeds darken, then add the turmeric, coriander and ground cumin. Cook for 15 seconds, stirring constantly. Stir in the onion and garlic purée and fry, scraping the pan with a spatula, until it begins to brown.

8 Return the potatoes and aubergines to the pan, season with salt, pepper and 1–2 pinches of cayenne. Add the remaining water and 15ml/1 tbsp lemon juice and then cook, stirring, until the liquid evaporates. Preheat the oven to 190°C/375°F/Gas 5.

9 Fill the peppers with the potato mixture and place on a lightly greased baking tray. Brush the peppers with a little oil and bake for 30–35 minutes, until the peppers are cooked. Allow to cool a little, then sprinkle with a little more lemon juice, garnish with the coriander and serve.

Cook's tip
Kalonji, or nigella as it is sometimes known, is a tiny black onion seed. It is widely used in Indian cookery, especially sprinkled over breads or in potato dishes. It has a mild, slightly nutty flavour and is best toasted for a few seconds in a dry frying pan over a medium heat.

Energy 234kcal/976kJ; Protein 4.2g; Carbohydrate 28.1g, of which sugars 14.8g; Fat 12.4g, of which saturates 2.4g; Cholesterol 0mg; Calcium 45mg; Fibre 5.5g; Sodium 21mg.

Beetroot with lemon dressing

Beetroot has been used as a food and medicine since early times. Its unique mixture of minerals and phytochemicals helps the body to resist infection, and may boost cellular oxygen and combat disorders of the immune system, blood and liver.

Serves 4

450g/1lb evenly sized raw beetroot (beets)
grated rind and juice of ½ lemon
about 150ml/¼ pint/⅔ cup extra virgin olive
    oil (or a mixture of olive and sunflower oil,
    blended to taste)
sea salt and ground black pepper
chopped fresh chives, to garnish (optional)

Cook's tip
To avoid the beetroots (beets) 'bleeding' during cooking, twist off the tops and discard them, rather than cutting them with a knife.

1 Twist off the tops from the beetroot (see Cook's tip), and cook in a large pan of salted boiling water for about 30 minutes, or until the beetroot is tender. Pinch the skin between two fingers: when cooked, the skin will come away easily.

2 Drain the beetroot and allow it to cool. Peel when cool and slice into wedges into a bowl.

3 Add the lemon rind and juice, and the oil; season to taste. Mix gently in the dressing and serve.

Energy 265kcal/1097kJ; Protein 1.9g; Carbohydrate 8.6g, of which sugars 7.9g; Fat 25.1g, of which saturates 3.6g; Cholesterol 0mg; Calcium 23mg; Fibre 2.2g; Sodium 74mg.

Apple and red beetroot salad

This combination of apple and beetroot makes an excellent cleanser of the blood and liver. These red fruits and vegetables are rich in vitamins C, E and betacarotene. They contain antioxidants, which can help to fight cell damage caused by harmful free radicals.

Serves 4

50g/2oz/⅓ cup whole shelled almonds
2 red apples, cored and diced
juice of ½ lemon
115g/4oz/4 cups red salad leaves, such as
    lollo rosso, oak leaf and radicchio
200g/7oz cooked beetroot (beets) in juice

For the dressing
30ml/2 tbsp olive oil
15ml/1 tbsp walnut oil
15ml/1 tbsp cider vinegar
freshly ground black pepper

Variation
Serve as a first course, adding a sprinkling of chopped chives.

1 Blanch the almonds in boiling water for 1 minute and skin them. Toast them in a dry frying pan for 2–3 minutes until golden brown, tossing frequently.

2 Meanwhile, make the dressing. Put the olive and walnut oils, cider vinegar and freshly ground black pepper in a bowl or screw-top jar. Stir or shake thoroughly to combine the ingredients.

3 Toss the diced apples in lemon juice to prevent them browning. Slice the beetroot. Then place the apples on a large serving platter or in a large bowl and add the salad leaves and beetroot.

4 Pour the dressing over the salad and toss gently, using your hands. Scatter the toasted almonds over the dressed salad and serve.

Energy 216kcal/895kJ; Protein 4.1g; Carbohydrate 9.5g, of which sugars 8.8g; Fat 18.2g, of which saturates 1.9g; Cholesterol 0mg; Calcium 54mg; Fibre 2.7g; Sodium 58mg.

Minted pomegranate yogurt with grapefruit salad

Many studies favour pomegranate seeds and juice, saying that they help with persistent cancer problems. Rich in vitamins A, B and C, it is considered a tonic for the heart, kidneys, bladder and liver. The juice is recommended for people with bladder disorders such as cystitis.

4 Discard the membranes and mix the fruit segments with the reserved fruit juices. Sprinkle the segments with the orange flower water and add a little honey or sugar, if using. Stir gently to mix, then decorate with a few pomegranate seeds.

5 Just before serving, decorate the chilled yogurt with a sprinkling of pomegranate seeds and mint leaves.

6 Serve the minted pomegranate yogurt with the grapefruit salad.

Variation
For a refreshing alternative, you can use a mixture of oranges and blood oranges, interspersed with thin segments of lemon. Lime segments work well with the grapefruit and mandarins or tangerines could be used too. As the idea is to create a refreshing, scented salad, juicy melons and kiwi fruit would also make an ideal combination.

Serves 3–4

300ml/½ pint/1¼ cups low-fat probiotic yogurt
2–3 ripe pomegranates
small bunch of fresh mint, finely chopped
clear honey or caster (superfine) sugar, to
    taste (optional)

For the grapefruit salad
2 red grapefruits
2 pink grapefruits
1 white grapefruit
15–30ml/1–2 tbsp orange flower water

To decorate
handful of pomegranate seeds
fresh mint leaves

1 Put the yogurt in a bowl and beat well. Cut open the pomegranates and scoop out the seeds, removing and discarding all the bitter pith. Fold the pomegranate seeds and chopped mint into the yogurt. Sweeten with a little honey or sugar, if using, then chill until ready to serve.

2 To make the salad, peel the red, pink and white grapefruits, cutting off and discarding all the pith.

3 Holding each fruit in the palm of your hand, cut between the membranes to remove the segments. Prepare the fruit over a bowl to catch the juices.

Energy 115kcal/482kJ; Protein 6g; Carbohydrate 21.7g, of which sugars 21.7g; Fat 1.1g, of which saturates 0.4g; Cholesterol 1mg; Calcium 210mg; Fibre 3.4g; Sodium 73mg.

Raspberry fromage frais and amaretti scrunch

This low-fat dessert contains raspberries to activate the body's natural self-cleansing ability and improve the health of the skin, hair, sweat glands, nerves and bone marrow. They enhance the healing of wounds, and their powerful antioxidant properties mean they protect against disease.

Serves 4

250g/9oz/1½ cups frozen or fresh raspberries
500g/1¼lb/2½ cups fromage frais or thick
　　natural (plain) live yogurt
30ml/2 tbsp clear honey
finely grated rind of 1 small lemon
75g/3oz/1½ cups amaretti biscuits, broken
　　into pieces
crystallized rose petals, for decoration
　　(optional)

1 If using frozen raspberries, allow them to partly defrost. If you are using fresh ones, partly freeze them.

2 Place the fromage frais or yogurt in a large bowl and stir in the honey and lemon rind. Add the raspberries and fold in gently, being careful not to over mix. Chill for 1 hour.

3 Stir the amaretti biscuits into the raspberry mixture just before serving.

4 Decorate with crystallized rose petals, if you wish.

Energy 183kcal/771kJ; Protein 5.7g; Carbohydrate 27.2g, of which sugars 21.3g; Fat 6.4g, of which saturates 3.7g; Cholesterol 17mg; Calcium 99mg; Fibre 1.2g; Sodium 72mg.

Strawberries with passion fruit

Rich in antioxidants, strawberries contain betacarotene and vitamin C, which helps to neutralize harmful free radicals in the body. These little berries can be used to relieve the symptoms of rheumatoid arthritis. They are great for promoting healthy skin and mucous membrane as well as encouraging iron absorption, reducing blood-fat levels and helping the body cope with stress.

Serves 4

350g/12oz raspberries, fresh or frozen
30ml/2 tbsp honey
1 passion fruit
700g/1½lb small strawberries

1 Place the raspberries and honey in a non-corrosive pan and warm over a very gentle heat to release the juices. When the juices start to run, simmer for 5 minutes, stirring occasionally. Set aside and allow the mixture to cool.

2 Halve the passion fruit and, using a teaspoon, carefully scoop out the seeds and juice into a small bowl.

3 Put the raspberries and passion fruit into a food processor, and blend until smooth. Press through a fine nylon sieve (strainer) to remove the seeds.

4 Place the strawberries in a bowl and serve with the sauce.

Cook's tip
Berry fruits offer their best flavour when served at room temperature.

Energy 92kcal/391kJ; Protein 2.8g; Carbohydrate 20.5g, of which sugars 20.5g; Fat 0.5g, of which saturates 0.1g; Cholesterol 0mg; Calcium 51mg; Fibre 4.2g; Sodium 15mg.

Rhubarb and ginger jellies

Rhubarb is a great tonic and laxative. It is a fruit with anti-parasitic properties that helps control the bile flow as well as preventing harmful bacteria in the gut. Rhubarb must be cooked to gain all the above properties, but remember to discard the leaves, which are poisonous. The ground-up root is used in tinctures to form a laxative.

Serves 5–6

1kg/2¼ lb young rhubarb
200g/7oz/1 cup caster (superfine) sugar
50g/2oz fresh root ginger, finely chopped
15ml/1 tbsp powdered gelatine

1 Cut the rhubarb into 2cm/¾in chunks and place in a pan with the sugar and ginger. Pour in 450ml/¾ pint/scant 2 cups water and bring to the boil. Reduce the heat, cover and simmer gently for 10 minutes, until the rhubarb is very soft and pulpy.

2 Meanwhile, sprinkle the gelatine over 30ml/2 tbsp cold water in a small heatproof bowl. Leave to stand, without stirring, for 5 minutes, until the gelatine has become sponge-like in texture.

3 Set the heatproof bowl over a small pan of hot water and simmer, stirring occasionally with a wooden spoon, until the gelatine has dissolved completely into a clear liquid. Remove the pan from the heat.

4 Strain the cooked rhubarb through a fine sieve (strainer) into a bowl. Stir in the dissolved gelatine until thoroughly mixed. Leave to cool slightly before pouring into serving glasses. Chill for at least 4 hours or overnight, until set.

Energy 152kcal/652kJ; Protein 3.8g; Carbohydrate 36.2g, of which sugars 36.2g; Fat 0.2g, of which saturates 0g; Cholesterol 0mg; Calcium 176mg; Fibre 2.4g; Sodium 12mg.

green

THE COLOUR OF BALANCE

Green fruits and vegetables have many health-giving properties that seem almost too good to be true. It is best to eat green vegetables raw or cooked for the minimum amount of time to prevent destroying their vitamin content. Broccoli, spinach and green leafy vegetables are all excellent for health. When cells of the body get inflamed the body produces proteins called kinins. Eating plenty of green fruit and vegetables is known to reduce kinin production and help keep inflammation under control. Always eat these products as soon as possible after purchasing or the nutritional values will start to deteriorate.

What green foods to eat

Green is for go. These colours are of harmony and sympathy and can make you feel more balanced if you prefer a quiet life away from stress. The brassica family of vegetables includes cabbages, broccoli and Brussels sprouts and are a good source of calcium, minerals, folic acid, iron, potassium and betacarotene. They contain a range of phytonutrients, which are important for health. They also have a variety of antioxidants that may help reduce the risk of bowel cancer and cardiovascular disease.

Green Vegetables

Asparagus provides vitamins A, B2 and C and is also a good source of potassium, iron and calcium. It is a well-known diuretic.

Avocados are rich in potassium, vitamin C, some B vitamins and especially vitamin E. Their rich oils, particularly the vitamin E content, mean that avocados are not only useful as food, but also for skin and hair care.

Broccoli is one of the superfoods that really does help promote good health. It is a very good source of calcium, which helps maintain strong bones, teeth and muscle. It is rich in indols and folic acid noted for its sulphoraphane content. It has

Below: Broccoli

phytochemicals, which have been shown to activate enzymes and help destroy cancer-causing chemicals. It is a good source of vitamins A and C and other antioxidants.

Brussels Sprouts are an excellent source of calcium, minerals, folic acid, iron, potassium and betacarotene. They contain phytonutrients and also antioxidants, which help to reduce the risk of bowel cancer and cardiovascular disease.

Celery contains potassium, which is essential for the functioning of all cells in our bodies, and calcium for healthy bones and teeth.

Chayote is a good source of vitamin C and fibre. It contains 40 times more folate than broccoli, one of the B vitamins known to help decrease homocysteine levels, a risk factor for heart disease.

Chinese Cabbage is a good source of vitamin A for healthy sight and bones, vitamin C, and antioxidant carotenoids.

Courgettes (Zucchini) are rich in minerals, vitamins, fibre, potassium and folic acid, which is helpful in pregnancy.

Below: Curly kale

Above: Cabbage

Cucumbers are high in potassium, which is useful in the treatment of blood pressure, and they are a natural diuretic.

Fennel is rich in vitamin A and contains useful amounts of calcium, phosphorus and potassium. It is said to improve eyesight and help hypertension.

French Beans (Green Beans) contain vitamin C, betacarotene and fibre, which can help prevent colon cancer. They also contain magnesium and potassium, which help lower high blood pressure.

Globe Artichokes are high in insoluble fibre, a natural laxative, and a good source of folic acid, which is important for women of child-bearing years and may help prevent heart disease.

Green Chillies contain a phytochemical known as capsaicin, which can help fight cancer, provide pain relief and prevent sinusitis.

Green Onions contain cycloallin, an anticoagulant, which helps protect against heart disease. They contain vitamins B and C as well as calcium, iron and potassium.

Green (Bell) Peppers are rich in phytochemicals that appear to provide anti-inflammatory benefits.

GREEN FOR GOOD HEALTH

Green ingredients are especially rich in antioxidants. They will strengthen the immune system, guard against infection, and may help your body fight allergies and reduce the risk of cancer.

Brussels sprouts
Green tea
Watercress
Broccoli
Cabbage
Spinach
Apples
Fennel
Curly kale
Kiwi
Green grapes
Samphire

Leafy Greens, including curly kale, endive and spring greens, are a rich source of minerals, including iron, calcium, potassium and magnesium, and vitamins K, C, E and B. Vitamin K is especially valuable since it may help prevent osteoporosis and regulate blood clotting. The darker-coloured greens are higher in betacarotene.

Leeks are a good source of dietary fibre and also contain folic acid, calcium, potassium and vitamin C. They have antiseptic, laxative, diuretic and anti-arthritic properties.

Lettuce and Salad Leaves are a good source of vitamins A, C and E. They provide potassium, iron and calcium and traces of other minerals. Lettuce can act as a soporific and help insomnia. It also aids digestion and is thought to promote liver health.

Mangetouts (Snowpeas) are a rich source of iron, to fortify the blood, and vitamin C, which helps support the immune system.

Okra is a good source of vitamins B6 and C, calcium, and folic acid.

Pak Choi (Bok Choy) contains powerful antioxidants, vitamins A and C and folic acid. It can aid digestion.

Peas are high in folic acid, vitamin B6 and vitamin K. They guard against osteoporosis and can aid good cardiovascular health.

Rocket (Arugula) is rich in phytonutrients, which protect the body from breast, stomach and colon cancers and are a good source of calcium, manganese and magnesium.

Spinach contains vitamin C if eaten raw, as well as vitamins A and B, calcium, potassium and iron.

Sugarsnap Peas contain iron and vitamin C, which helps build the immune system.

Watercress is extremely rich in vitamins A, B2, C, D and E. It also provides significant quantities of calcium, iron, potassium and sulphur.

Wheatgrass is a good source of fibre and iron. It may promote a general sense of well-being, have antibacterial properties and aid in digestion.

Green Fruits

Gooseberries are especially high in vitamin C and also contain vitamins A and D, potassium, calcium, phosphorus and niacin. They are rich in dietary fibre, which may help guard against cancer.

Green Apples, including eating and cooking apples, contain useful quantities of

Above: Limes

vitamins C and A. They are high in pectin and a good source of dietary fibre.

Green Grapes contain small amounts of vitamin A, minerals, including potassium and iron, and dietary fibre.

Green Pears contain a small amount of vitamins A and C and some potassium and riboflavin, which aids normal cell function, growth and energy production.

Kiwi Fruit are very high in vitamin C, which promotes tissue repair and is an antioxidant and plays an important role in the absorption of iron and the formation of antibodies.

Limes are rich in vitamin C, and contain some potassium, calcium and phosphorus. They guard against all kinds of ills including digestive disorders and constipation, peptic ulcers, gum disease, respiratory disorders, urinary infections and scurvy.

Papayas are rich in vitamin A and calcium, and contain large quantities of the enzyme papain, which breaks down protein and is used to tenderize meat. Papain makes fruit easy to digest.

Left: Apple

Below: Grapes

Health benefits of green foods

Green-coloured fruit and vegetables are rich in vitamins, potassium, sulphur and copper as well as antioxidants, which help to reduce the risk of bowel cancer and cardiovascular disease. Green fruits and vegetables are a good source of anti-inflammatory and diuretic substances and help to regulate blood sugar levels. Medical uses of the cabbage family focus on digestive ailments like colitis, stomach ulcers and gastritis. The green pigment in fruits and vegetables contain varying amounts of phytochemicals such as lutein and indoles, and have potential antioxidant, health-promoting benefits. Green food in the diet helps to lower the risk of some cancers, and also gives us better vision and strengthens bones and teeth.

Many green fruits and vegetables, including avocado, broccoli and leafy greens contain vitamins A, C, E and B. They have diuretic properties, which help kidney function and prevent water retention. Rich in antioxidants, they can strengthen the immune system and help the body overcome infections.

Most greens are believed to reduce the risk of certain cancers, including lung and colon cancer. The brassica family is packed full of minerals like glucosinolates, and claimed to be anti-allergic, anti-cancer, detoxifying and immuno-stimulant. When making sandwiches, add lovely crispy salads and herbs to help give them extra vitamins and potassium.

The Colour of Balance

Choose foods from this group at times of the day when you feel anxious or need to calm down. Green fruit and vegetables can promote a feeling of tranquillity. Make sure that your diet is as varied and colourful as possible. Buy local seasonal fruit and vegetables since these are often more valuable nutritionally.

Chlorophyll is found in every green plant from spinach to gooseberries. It acts in an antibacterial and anti-inflammatory way as well as purifying the blood from toxins and other waste that could poison the body.

The green pigment also indicates the presence of lutein, which improves eyesight, the skeleton and teeth and helps protect organs from cancer. Lutein is found in many green vegetables, herbs and fruit, including cabbages, peas, spinach, lettuce, nettles, kiwi fruit, green apples, green tea, asparagus as well as wheatgrass and other plant foods. Lutein is very concentrated in the macula of the eyes so green leafy vegetables are valuable for people with eye problems or those over-exposed to sun rays or using computer screens.

Other Benefits

Experts all agree that eating more raw fresh fruits and vegetables is the way forward to help to combat certain illnesses. The phytonutrients found in the cruciferous family, such as Brussels sprouts and cabbage, are thought to help fight off some types of cancer,

Left: Spinach

including those of the stomach and colon. Sprouts are also rich in folic acid, the lack of which is associated with heart disease and Alzheimer's disease.

The white pigment in many vegetables, including cabbage stalks, core and ribs, contains more than one antioxidant. For example, garlic contains anthocyanins.

Broccoli is an excellent source of calcium, for healthy strong bones, teeth and muscle, making it an option for those who cannot eat dairy foods.

Below: Brussels sprouts

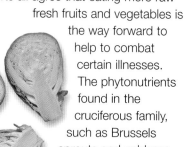

GREEN FOODS FOR HEALTH

Leafy salads are low in calories yet high in all kinds of minerals and phytonutrients. Make use of them every day to help you combine a healthy diet and lifestyle. Scientists predict that by the end of 2020 one in four of us will be obese. Salads can help you maintain a healthy weight, and weight control plus being physically active can reduce illness by some 35 per cent. Broccoli, spinach, green apples and other top superfoods in your diet will give you a better chance of achieving and maintaining a healthy body and avoiding the risk of heart attack and cancer.

Above: Fennel

Below: Gooseberries

Above: Green and leafy salads are packed with goodness and powerful antioxidants for healthy living.

Above: Kiwi fruit

The majority of green vegetables contain folic acid, iron, potassium, vitamin C and betacarotene. The darker green in colour the vegetables, the richer in nutrients they will be. Make sure that vegetables are not overcooked to avoid destroying the valuable vitamin C.

Spinach, especially raw spinach, is rich in iron, but it does take a long time to be absorbed into your blood stream compared with other iron-rich foods.

Look out on the supermarket shelves for lots of new green vegetables and shoots, not forgetting the wonderful array of mixed salad leaves, herbs and watercresses containing phytonutrients.

Right: Broccoli

Wheatgrass tonic

It is claimed that wheatgrass helps combat tiredness and body fatigue. It is a very concentrated form of chlorophyll, being an immune-enhancing nutrient and powerful liver detoxifier. It stimulates haemoglobin production, lowers cholesterol and helps regulate blood fat levels. This health drink contains vitamin A and E as well as antioxidants, zinc and fibre.

Makes 1 small glass

50g/2oz white cabbage
90g/3½oz wheatgrass

1 Using a small, sharp knife, roughly shred the cabbage.

2 Push through a juicer with the wheatgrass. Pour the juice into a small glass and serve immediately.

Energy 36kcal/149kJ; Protein 3.2g; Carbohydrate 3.9g, of which sugars 3.8g; Fat 0.8g, of which saturates 0.1g; Cholesterol 0mg; Calcium 178mg; Fibre 2.9g; Sodium 130mg.

Green devil

Avocados are rich in potassium for fatigue, depression and poor digestion. They are also rich in vitamins A, B, C and E. They contain very healthy monounsaturated oil, which stimulates production of collagen and contains unsaturated fatty acid. Avocados are packed with energy and immune-boosting phytochemicals, which can guard against fungal diseases and cancer.

Makes 2–3 glasses

1 small ripe avocado
½ cucumber
30ml/2 tbsp lemon juice
30ml/2 tbsp lime juice
10ml/2 tsp caster (superfine) sugar
pinch of salt
250ml/8fl oz/1 cup apple juice or
    mineral water
10–20ml/2–4 tsp sweet chilli sauce
ice cubes
red chilli curls, to decorate

2 Process the ingredients until smooth and creamy, then add the apple juice or mineral water and a little of the chilli sauce. Blend once more to lightly mix the ingredients together.

3 Pour the smoothie over ice cubes. Decorate with red chilli curls and serve with stirrers and extra chilli sauce.

1 Halve the avocado and use a sharp knife to remove the stone (pit). Scoop the flesh from both halves into a blender or food processor. Peel and roughly chop the cucumber and add to the blender or food processor, then add the lemon and lime juice, the caster sugar and a little salt.

Cook's tips

To make chilli curls, core and seed a fresh red chilli and cut it into very fine strips. Put the strips in a bowl of iced water and leave to stand for 20 minutes or until the strips curl. Use them to decorate this smoothie.

Seductively smooth avocados are as good for you as they taste. Their fresh vitamin- and mineral-rich flesh is reputed to be fantastic for healthy hair and skin.

Energy 143kcal/598kJ; Protein 1.3g; Carbohydrate 13.2g, of which sugars 12.5g; Fat 9.8g, of which saturates 2.1g; Cholesterol 0mg; Calcium 19mg; Fibre 1.9g; Sodium 6mg.

Cold cucumber and yogurt soup

Cucumbers have a very high water content. They are a diuretic and anti-inflammatory, which helps to dissolve uric acid and intestinal health. Eat cucumbers with the skin on as it contains all the nutrients and fibre. Rich in vitamins A, B and C, they can help with problems such as gout, rheumatism and ulcerative colitis. Walnuts are an astringent and may lower cholesterol levels.

Serves 5–6

1 cucumber
4 garlic cloves
2.5ml/½ tsp salt
75g/3oz/¾ cup shelled walnut pieces
40g/1½oz day-old bread, torn into pieces
30ml/2 tbsp walnut or sunflower oil
400ml/14fl oz/1⅔ cups cow's or
   sheep's yogurt
120ml/4fl oz/½ cup cold water or chilled
   still mineral water
5–10ml/1–2 tsp lemon juice

For the garnish
40g/1½oz/scant ½ cup shelled walnuts,
   coarsely chopped
25ml/1½ tbsp olive oil
sprigs of fresh dill

1 Cut the cucumber into 2 and peel one half of it. Discard the peel. Dice the flesh of the whole cucumber into small pieces and set aside.

2 Peel the garlic. Using a large mortar and pestle, crush the garlic and salt together well; then add the walnuts and bread and pound together.

3 When the mixture is smooth, add the walnut or sunflower oil slowly and combine well.

4 Transfer the mixture into a large bowl and beat in the yogurt and the diced cucumber.

5 Add the cold water or mineral water, stirring thoroughly, and then add lemon juice to taste.

6 Pour the soup into chilled soup bowls to serve. Garnish with the coarsely chopped walnuts, a little olive oil drizzled over the nuts and sprigs of fresh dill.

Energy 220kcal/910kJ; Protein 6.9g; Carbohydrate 9.2g, of which sugars 5.9g; Fat 17.6g, of which saturates 1.9g; Cholesterol 1mg; Calcium 155mg; Fibre 0.9g; Sodium 92mg.

Pea soup with garlic

Peas are a good source of soluble dietary fibre. In recent tests it has been proven they lower cholesterol levels. They are high in vitamin C and rich in folic acid, iron, phosphorus and protein. This vegetable is a good energy-providing food, which has tonic properties in helping to regulate bowel and digestive functions.

Serves 4

25g/1oz/2 tbsp butter
1 garlic clove, crushed
900g/2lb/8 cups frozen peas
1.2 litres/2 pints/5 cups chicken stock
salt and ground black pepper

1 Heat the butter in a large pan and add the garlic. Fry gently for 2–3 minutes or until softened, then add the peas. Cook for 1–2 minutes more, then pour in the stock.

Cook's tip
Keep a bag of frozen peas in the freezer, for a quick and easy supper.

2 Bring the soup to the boil, then reduce the heat to a simmer. Cover and cook for 5–6 minutes, until the peas are tender. Leave to cool slightly, then transfer the mixture to a food processor and process until smooth (you may have to do this in two batches).

3 Return the soup to the pan and heat through gently. Season with salt and pepper to taste.

Energy 233kcal/965kJ; Protein 15.6g; Carbohydrate 25.5g, of which sugars 5.2g; Fat 8.5g, of which saturates 3.9g; Cholesterol 13mg; Calcium 49mg; Fibre 10.6g; Sodium 40mg.

Pea guacamole with crudités

This low-fat appetizer is very healthy and nutritious served with fresh crunchy vegetables. Peas are a good source of energy, and they are high in dietary fibre, which has gastronic properties that help the bowel function. Both the peas and the lime juice are rich in vitamin C.

Serves 4

350g/12oz/3 cups frozen peas, completely defrosted
1 garlic clove, crushed
2 spring onions (scallions), trimmed and chopped
5ml/1 tsp finely grated rind and juice of 1 lime
2.5ml/½ tsp ground cumin
dash of Tabasco sauce
15ml/1 tbsp extra virgin olive oil
30ml/2 tbsp chopped fresh coriander (cilantro)
freshly ground black pepper
pinch of cayenne and lime wedges, to garnish

For the crudités
6 baby carrots
2 celery sticks
1 red-skinned eating apple
1 pear
15ml/1 tbsp lemon or lime juice
6 baby corn

1 Put the peas, garlic, spring onions, lime rind and juice, cumin, Tabasco sauce, olive oil and freshly ground black pepper into a food processor or a blender and process for a few minutes until smooth.

2 Add the chopped fresh coriander and process for a few more seconds. Spoon into a serving bowl, cover with clear film (plastic wrap) and place in the refrigerator to chill for about 30 minutes.

3 To make the crudités, trim and peel the carrots and quarter lengthways. Halve the celery sticks lengthways and trim to the same length as the carrots. Quarter, core and thickly slice the apple and pear, then dip into the lemon or lime juice. Arrange with the baby corn in a bowl or on a platter.

4 Remove the clear film, sprinkle the cayenne over the guacamole and garnish with the lime wedges.

Energy 103kcal/425kJ; Protein 6.5g; Carbohydrate 10.4g, of which sugars 2.5g; Fat 4.3g, of which saturates 0.7g; Cholesterol 0mg; Calcium 45mg; Fibre 4.8g; Sodium 5mg.

Mixed green leaf and herb salad

Fresh salad leaves and herbs have mild diuretic properties and contain a bitterish compound good for the liver and gall bladder. This salad is mixed with a plain olive oil dressing that is an antioxidant and a monounsaturated fat as well as being rich in vitamin E.

Serves 4

15g/½oz/½ cup mixed fresh herbs, such
    as chervil, tarragon (use sparingly), dill,
    basil, marjoram (use sparingly), lemon-
    scented thyme, flat leaf parsley, mint,
    sorrel, fennel and coriander (cilantro)
350g/12oz mixed salad leaves, such as
    rocket, radicchio, chicory, watercress,
    curly endive, baby spinach, oakleaf lettuce,
    nasturtium (and the flowers) and dandelion

For the dressing
50ml/2fl oz/¼ cup extra virgin olive oil
15ml/1 tbsp lemon juice
freshly ground black pepper

1 Wash and dry the herbs and salad leaves in a salad spinner, or use two clean, dry dish towels to pat them dry.

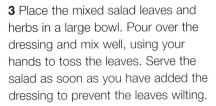

2 In a small bowl, blend together the olive oil and lemon juice and season with freshly ground black pepper to taste.

3 Place the mixed salad leaves and herbs in a large bowl. Pour over the dressing and mix well, using your hands to toss the leaves. Serve the salad as soon as you have added the dressing to prevent the leaves wilting.

Cook's tip
Nasturtiums and dandelions have a very strong taste, and dandelions have powerful diuretic properties, so they should be used in small quantities. The nasturtium flowers have great decorative value.

Variations
You can add any number of other ingredients to this salad for added substance, colour contrast and extra nutritional value. Try adding some of the following combinations of ingredients:
• Fresh tomatoes or (bell) peppers.
• Tiny new potatoes in their jackets, crumbled hard-boiled egg yolks and sprouted beansprouts.
• Baby broad (fava) beans, sliced artichoke hearts and bulgur wheat.
• Cooked chickpeas, asparagus tips and stoned green olives.

Energy 92kcal/377kJ; Protein 0.7g; Carbohydrate 1.6g, of which sugars 1.6g; Fat 9.2g, of which saturates 1.4g; Cholesterol 0mg; Calcium 26mg; Fibre 0.8g; Sodium 3mg.

Spinach and roast garlic salad

Spinach is rich in calcium and magnesium, which is needed by the muscles that help to digest food through the intestine, making this an ideal vegetable for constipation. It is a good source of carotenoids and when eaten regularly, might help to reduce the risk of heart disease and various cancers. Garlic is an antioxidant, which may ward off cell damage, too.

Serves 4

12 garlic cloves, unpeeled
60ml/4 tbsp extra virgin olive oil
450g/1lb baby spinach leaves
50g/2oz/½ cup pine nuts, lightly toasted
juice of ½ lemon
freshly ground black pepper

Cook's tip
If spinach is to be served raw in a salad, then the leaves need to be young and tender. Wash them well, drain and pat them dry with kitchen paper. Spinach offers the greatest health benefits when eaten raw as in this recipe.

1 Preheat the oven to 190°C/375°F/ Gas 5. Place the unpeeled garlic cloves in a small roasting dish, drizzle over 30ml/2 tbsp of the olive oil and toss to coat evenly.

2 Bake for about 15 minutes until the garlic cloves become slightly charred around the edges.

3 While still warm, put the garlic cloves, still in their skins, into a salad bowl. Add the spinach, pine nuts, lemon juice and remaining olive oil. Toss well and season with pepper to taste.

4 Serve immediately, letting the diners squeeze the softened garlic purée out of the skins.

Energy 238kcal/980kJ; Protein 6.9g; Carbohydrate 6.4g, of which sugars 2.6g; Fat 20.6g, of which saturates 2.3g; Cholesterol 0mg; Calcium 198mg; Fibre 3.6g; Sodium 159mg.

Broccoli with soy sauce

Broccoli is rich in indols and folic acid, noted for its sulphoraphane content. It contains phytochemicals, which have been shown to activate enzymes and help destroy cancer-causing chemicals. It is a good source of vitamins A and C and other antioxidants. Avoid over-cooking the broccoli since this can destroy some of its beneficial qualities.

Serves 4

450g/1lb broccoli
15ml/1 tbsp sunflower oil
2 garlic cloves, crushed
15ml/1 tbsp reduced-salt soy sauce
fried garlic slices, to garnish (optional)

1 Trim off the thick stems from the broccoli and cut the head part into large florets.

Variation
Replace the fried garlic slices and soy sauce with Japanese pickled ginger (gari) and 15ml/1 tbsp teriyaki sauce.

2 Bring a pan of water to the boil. Add the broccoli and cook for 3–4 minutes or until just tender.

3 Drain the broccoli thoroughly through a sieve (strainer) and arrange it in a heated serving dish.

4 Heat the sunflower oil in a small pan. Fry the garlic for 2 minutes, then remove with a slotted spoon. Pour the oil carefully over the broccoli.

5 Drizzle with soy sauce, scatter with fried garlic slices, if you like, and serve.

Energy 135kcal/558kJ; Protein 6.6g; Carbohydrate 2.7g, of which sugars 2.3g; Fat 10.9g, of which saturates 1.7g; Cholesterol 0mg; Calcium 115mg; Fibre 3.5g; Sodium 545mg.

Persian omelette

Spinach has many good qualities. It is rich in antioxidants, including betacarotene, which stimulates the pancreas function. Avoid eating too much spinach though if you suffer from gout or arthritis, as this can reduce the absorption of calcium and can inflame the digestive tract. Nuts and spinach are both a good source of omega-3.

3 Beat the eggs in a bowl with a fork. Add the leek and spinach mixture (or the leeks with the thawed frozen spinach), then stir in the spring onions, with all the herbs and nuts. Season with salt and pepper. Pour the mixture into the pan and cover with a lid or foil.

4 Cook over a very gentle heat for 25 minutes or until set. Remove the lid and brown the top under a hot grill. Serve, with salad.

Serves 8

30ml/2 tbsp olive oil or sunflower oil
2 leeks, finely chopped
350g/12oz fresh spinach, washed and chopped, or 150g/5oz thawed frozen chopped spinach, drained
12 eggs
8 spring onions (scallions), finely chopped
2 handfuls fresh parsley, finely chopped
1–2 handfuls fresh coriander (cilantro), chopped
2 fresh tarragon sprigs, chopped, or 2.5ml /½ tsp dried tarragon
handful of fresh chives, chopped
1 small fresh dill sprig, chopped, or 1.5ml /¼ tsp dried dill
2–4 fresh mint sprigs, chopped
40g/1½oz/⅓ cup walnuts or pecan nuts, chopped
40g/1½oz/½ cup pine nuts
sea salt and ground black pepper
salad, to serve

1 Heat the oil in a large shallow pan that can be used under the grill (broiler). Add the finely chopped leeks and fry them gently for about 5 minutes until they are just beginning to soften but not brown.

2 If using fresh spinach, add it to the pan containing the leeks and cook together for 2–3 minutes over a medium heat until the spinach has just wilted.

Energy 258kcals/1073kJ; Fat, total 21g; saturated fat 3.9g; polyunsaturated fat 6.1g; monounsaturated fat 8.7g; Carbohydrate 2.8g; sugar, total 2.3g; starch 0.15g; Fibre 1.9g; Sodium 192mg.

Courgette fritters with pistou

Courgettes contain a mild laxative and diuretic and can alleviate bladder or kidney infections, helping to prevent inflammation. They are rich in vitamins C and B and carotenes, and help maintain a good nervous system as well as helping prevent insomnia and gastroenteritis. Basil contains an essential oil that has antispasmodic and antiseptic properties.

Serves 4

For the pistou
4 garlic cloves, peeled and sliced
15g/½oz basil leaves
90g/3½oz/1 cup grated Parmesan cheese
finely grated rind of 1 lemon
150ml/¼ pint/⅔ cup olive oil

For the fritters
450g/1lb courgettes (zucchini), grated
75g/3oz/⅔ cup flour
1 egg, separated
15ml/1 tbsp olive oil
olive oil for shallow frying
salt and ground black pepper

1 To make the pistou, crush the garlic with a pestle and mortar, until it is reduced to a fairly fine paste.

2 Transfer the garlic paste to a food processor or blender. Add the basil leaves, grated cheese and lemon rind and process briefly. Gradually blend in the oil, a little at a time, until combined, then transfer to a small serving dish.

3 To make the fritters, put the courgettes in a sieve (strainer) over a bowl and sprinkle with salt. Leave for 1 hour, then rinse thoroughly. Dry on kitchen towels.

4 Sift the flour into a bowl. Add the egg yolk and oil, then gradually whisk in 75ml/5 tbsp water to make a smooth batter. Season and leave the batter to stand for 30 minutes.

5 Stir the drained courgettes into the batter. Whisk the egg white until stiff, then fold into the batter.

6 Heat 1cm/½in olive oil in a frying pan. Add spoonfuls of batter to the oil and fry for 2 minutes until golden, turning once. Drain the fritters on kitchen paper and keep warm while frying the rest. Serve with the sauce.

Energy 157kcal/652kJ; Protein 4.4g; Carbohydrate 11.1g, of which sugars 6.1g; Fat 10.8g, of which saturates 2.2g; Cholesterol 36mg; Calcium 85mg; Fibre 1.2g; Sodium 59mg.

Chilled stuffed courgettes

This ideal recipe for a light snack or lunch is low in fat and calories. Courgettes are rich in folic acid, which is helpful in pregnancy. Courgette flesh mashed down can make a wonderful face mask that can remedy inflammation from the skin and abscesses.

Serves 6

6 courgettes (zucchini)
1 Spanish onion, very finely chopped
1 garlic clove, crushed
60–90ml/4–6 tbsp well-flavoured
   French dressing
1 green (bell) pepper
3 tomatoes, peeled and seeded
15ml/1 tbsp rinsed capers
5ml/1 tsp chopped fresh parsley
5ml/1 tsp chopped fresh basil
sea salt and ground black pepper
parsley sprigs, to garnish

1 Top and tail the courgettes, but do not peel them. Bring a large shallow pan of lightly salted water to the boil, add the courgettes and simmer for 2–3 minutes until they are lightly cooked. Drain well and cool under running water.

2 Cut the courgettes in half lengthways. Carefully scoop out the flesh, discarding the seeds but leaving the shells intact, and chop the flesh into small cubes.

3 Place the chopped flesh in a bowl and cover with half the chopped onion. Dot with the crushed garlic. Drizzle 30ml/2 tbsp of the dressing over, cover and marinate for 2–3 hours.

4 Wrap the courgette shells tightly in clear film (plastic wrap), and chill them in the refrigerator until they are required.

5 Cut the pepper in half and remove the core and seeds. Dice the flesh.

Cook's tip
This recipe works well with all kinds of vegetables including marrow, squashes and (bell) peppers. Simmer the vegetable in a large pan of salted water until softened, then drain, cool under running water and stuff in the usual way.

6 Chop the tomatoes and capers finely. Stir the pepper, tomatoes and capers into the courgette mixture, with the remaining onion and the chopped herbs. Season with salt and pepper. Pour over enough of the remaining dressing to moisten the mixture and toss well.

7 Spoon the filling into the courgette shells, arrange on a platter and serve garnished with sprigs of parsley.

Energy 95kcals/390kJ; Fat, total 7.3g; saturated fat 1.1g; polyunsaturated fat 0.9g; monounsaturated fat 4.9g; Carbohydrate 5.3g; sugar, total 4.75g; starch 0.2g; Fibre 1.95g; Sodium 60mg.

Poached pears in scented honey syrup

Pears are a laxative, diuretic and astringent and they have a calming quality. They aid uric acid elimination and prevent harmful bacteria proliferating in the intestines. They contain minerals such as copper, iodine and zinc and are ideal for pregnant women and elderly people. Honey is a natural antibiotic that works internally and externally as well as aiding respiration.

Serves 4

45ml/3 tbsp clear honey
juice of 1 lemon
250ml/8fl oz/1 cup water
pinch of saffron threads
1 cinnamon stick
2–3 dried lavender heads
4 firm green pears

Cook's tip
Choose pears of similar size, with unmarked flesh and the stalks intact, for the most attractive appearance when served.

1 Heat the honey and lemon juice in a heavy pan that will hold the pears snugly. Stir over a gentle heat until the honey has dissolved. Add the water, saffron threads, cinnamon stick and flowers from 1–2 lavender heads. Bring the mixture to the boil, then reduce the heat and simmer for 5 minutes.

2 Peel the pears carefully, leaving the stalks attached. Add the pears to the pan and simmer for 20 minutes, turning and basting at regular intervals, until they are tender. Leave the pears to cool in the syrup and serve at room temperature, decorated with a few lavender flowers.

Energy 93kcal/392kJ; Protein 0.5g; Carbohydrate 23.6g, of which sugars 23.6g; Fat 0.2g, of which saturates 0g; Cholesterol 0mg; Calcium 17mg; Fibre 3.3g; Sodium 6mg.

Baked stuffed apples

Apples are rich in vitamin C and pectin, which is a gentle diuretic that aids in the elimination of uric acid and may help lower cholesterol levels in the blood. They are good for constipation, dyspepsia and peptic ulcers. They also help the symptoms of gout and rheumatoid arthritis, and may ease bowel problems.

Serves four

4 large cooking apples
75g/3oz/½ cup light muscovado (brown) sugar
75g/3oz/⅓ cup butter, softened
grated rind and juice of ½ orange
1.5ml/¼ tsp ground cinnamon
30ml/2 tbsp crushed ratafia biscuits
50g/2oz/½ cup shelled pecan nuts, chopped
50g/2oz/½ cup luxury mixed glacé
   (candied) fruit, chopped

Cook's tip
Pour a small amount of water around the apples to stop them sticking to the dish during baking.

1 Preheat the oven to 180°C/350°F/ Gas 4. Wash and dry the apples. Remove the cores with an apple corer, then carefully enlarge each core cavity to twice its size, by shaving off more flesh with the corer. Score each apple around its equator, using a sharp knife. Stand the apples in a baking dish.

2 Mix the sugar, butter, orange rind and juice, cinnamon and ratafia crumbs. Beat well, then stir in the nuts and glacé fruit. Divide the filling among the apples, piling it high. Shield the filling in each apple with a small piece of foil. Bake for 45–60 minutes until each apple is tender.

Energy 294kcal/1229kJ; Protein 5.3g; Carbohydrate 22.8g, of which sugars 22.2g; Fat 20.9g, of which saturates 6.2g; Cholesterol 21mg; Calcium 66mg; Fibre 4.1g; Sodium 67mg.

Ginger and kiwi sorbet

Kiwis are green when they are ripe and a valuable source of vitamins A, C and K. Kiwis are also rich in potassium and magnesium and have a good shelf-life. Their colour is due to the photo-chemical chlorophyll. They encourage the health and repair of all body tissues as well as helping to promote the release of the energy from other foods.

2 Peel the kiwi fruit and blend until smooth. Add the purée to the chilled syrup and mix well.

3 by hand: Pour the mixture into a container and freeze for 3–4 hours, beating twice as it thickens. Return to the freezer until ready to serve.

using an ice cream maker: Churn the kiwi and ginger mixture until it thickens. Transfer to a plastic tub or similar freezerproof container and freeze until ready to serve.

4 Transfer the sorbet to the refrigerator for 10 minutes before serving, to soften it slightly. Spoon into bowls or glasses, decorate with mint sprigs or chopped kiwi fruit, and serve.

Serves 6

150g/2oz fresh root ginger
115g/4oz/½ cup caster (superfine) sugar
300ml/½ pint/1¼ cups water
5 kiwi fruit
fresh mint sprigs or chopped kiwi fruit,
   to decorate

Cook's tip
Choose plump unwrinkled fruit with unblemished skins. Kiwis are ripe when they yield to gentle pressure like a ripe pear.

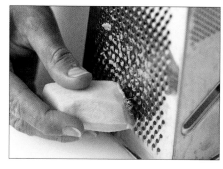

1 Peel the ginger and grate it finely. Put the sugar and water in a pan and heat gently until the sugar has dissolved. Add the ginger and cook for 1 minute, then leave to cool. Strain into a bowl and chill until very cold.

Energy 100kcal/426kJ; Protein 0.7g; Carbohydrate 25.3g, of which sugars 25.2g; Fat 0.3g, of which saturates 0g; Cholesterol 0mg; Calcium 23mg; Fibre 1g; Sodium 3mg.

Gooseberry and elderflower sorbet

These little green berries are a laxative and diuretic. They are thought to stimulate liver function and can ease inflammation of the digestive and urinary tracts. Gooseberries are rich in vitamins A, B and C, iron, natural sugars and malic and citric acid. They help alleviate the symptoms of sufferers from gout and rheumatoid arthritis.

Serves 6

150g/5oz/⅔ cup caster (superfine) sugar
175ml/6fl oz/¾ cup water
10 elderflower heads, plus extra to decorate
500g/1¼lb/5 cups gooseberries
200ml/7fl oz/scant 1 cup apple juice
dash of green food colouring (optional)
a little beaten egg white and caster
 (superfine) sugar, to decorate

1 Put 30ml/2 tbsp of the sugar in a pan with 30ml/2 tbsp of the water. Set aside. Mix the remaining sugar and water in a separate pan. Heat gently, stirring, until the sugar dissolves. Bring to the boil and boil for 1 minute, without stirring, to make a syrup.

2 Place the elderflower heads in a sieve (strainer) and rinse well with cold water. Allow to drain.

3 Add the elderflower heads and gooseberries to the sugar syrup in the pan. Cook gently for about 5 minutes.

4 Transfer to a food processor and add the apple juice. Process until smooth, then press through a sieve into a bowl. Leave to cool. Stir in the green food colouring if using. Chill until very cold.

5 by hand: Pour the mixture into a shallow container and freeze until thick, preferably overnight.

using an ice cream maker: Churn the mixture until it holds its shape. Transfer to a freezerproof container and freeze for several hours or overnight.

6 To decorate the glasses, put a little egg white in a shallow bowl and a thin layer of caster sugar on a flat plate. Dip the rim of each glass in the egg white, then the sugar to coat evenly. Leave to dry. Scoop the sorbet into the glasses, decorate with elderflowers and serve.

Energy 127kcal/542kJ; Protein 1.1g; Carbohydrate 31.9g, of which sugars 31.9g; Fat 0.4g, of which saturates 0g; Cholesterol 0mg; Calcium 39mg; Fibre 2g; Sodium 4mg.

blue and purple

THE HEALING FOODS

Many blue and purple fresh fruits and vegetables are called healing foods. They contain such phytochemicals as anthocyanins and phenolics as well as antioxidants. Blueberries, aubergines and blackcurrants may have anti-ageing qualities and also promote speedy recovery after illness. They are also believed to have antibacterial benefits, which help maintain healthy intestines, circulatory and urinary systems and memory function.

What blue & purple foods to eat

These colours symbolize peace and restfulness. Blue and purple foods will bring you calm and help you get a good night's sleep. Eating blue food such as blueberries is really beneficial as they heal from the inside out and are a true superfood, helping balance, coordination, bowel function, circulation and eyesight. Berries can be stored in the refrigerator for up to a week and are great for snacking or giving a kick start first thing in the morning.

Blue and purple fruits and vegetables contain varying amounts of health-promoting phytochemicals such as anthocyanins and phenolics, currently being studied for their anti-ageing and antioxidant benefits. All such fruits and vegetables help in the natural detoxification of the body, while providing a healthy balance of nutrients. Blueberries, blackcurrants, bilberries and other berries are thought to be useful in the prevention of cancer and other degenerative diseases.

Blue and Purple Vegetables

Aubergines (Eggplants) have a dark skin that contains anthocyanins, which are powerful antioxidants, guarding against strokes and heart disease. They

Below: Purple garlic

Below: Aubergines

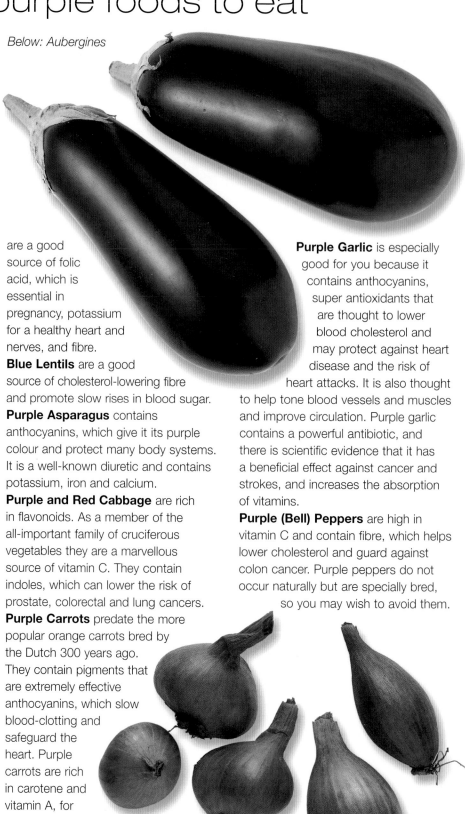

are a good source of folic acid, which is essential in pregnancy, potassium for a healthy heart and nerves, and fibre.

Blue Lentils are a good source of cholesterol-lowering fibre and promote slow rises in blood sugar.

Purple Asparagus contains anthocyanins, which give it its purple colour and protect many body systems. It is a well-known diuretic and contains potassium, iron and calcium.

Purple and Red Cabbage are rich in flavonoids. As a member of the all-important family of cruciferous vegetables they are a marvellous source of vitamin C. They contain indoles, which can lower the risk of prostate, colorectal and lung cancers.

Purple Carrots predate the more popular orange carrots bred by the Dutch 300 years ago. They contain pigments that are extremely effective anthocyanins, which slow blood-clotting and safeguard the heart. Purple carrots are rich in carotene and vitamin A, for good eye health.

Purple Belgian Endive is a good source of vitamins A and C and dietary fibre. Its bitter juice stimulates the appetite, and may help cases of anorexia and gastric and digestive problems.

Purple Garlic is especially good for you because it contains anthocyanins, super antioxidants that are thought to lower blood cholesterol and may protect against heart disease and the risk of heart attacks. It is also thought to help tone blood vessels and muscles and improve circulation. Purple garlic contains a powerful antibiotic, and there is scientific evidence that it has a beneficial effect against cancer and strokes, and increases the absorption of vitamins.

Purple (Bell) Peppers are high in vitamin C and contain fibre, which helps lower cholesterol and guard against colon cancer. Purple peppers do not occur naturally but are specially bred, so you may wish to avoid them.

Above: Shallots

Below: Blackberries

Above: Cherries
Left: Plums

Above: Blueberries

Purple Potatoes are a good source of vitamin C, especially during the winter. They also contain potassium, iron and vitamin B.
Shallots contain flavonoids, which help reduce the chance of developing cancer and heart disease, and are good at helping the liver eliminate toxins from the body. They are high in vitamin C and potassium and are anti-inflammatory, antiviral and anti-allergenic.

Blue and Purple Fruits

Aronia Berries are high in antioxidants, which help protect the body against cancer, and contain vitamins C, E and folic acid.

Below: Purple figs

Blackberries are rich in dietary fibre and vitamin C and are often used to make health drinks. They contain some calcium, phosphorus and potassium.
Blackcurrants are high in vitamin C, which helps the body fight cold and flu symptoms. They also contain potassium, which can help as a tonic and lower blood pressure.
Blueberries and Bilberries are high in antioxidants, which help fight cancer, especially colon lesions and ovarian cancer. Their enzymes can help reverse memory loss and slow down osteoporosis.
Elderberries are an excellent source of vitamin C, which promotes tissue repair and wound healing and in the general health of the immune system.
Passion Fruit contain vitamins A and C, as well as potassium and iron, and are a good source of dietary fibre.
Plums and Damsons are super-rich in antioxidants, containing more than any other fruit. They help keep a healthy heart and reduce blood cholesterol.
Prunes contain all the health benefits of plums, being high in antioxidants and fibre. They can help slow the ageing processes and in cases of anaemia.
Purple Figs are a good source of calcium and are high in fibre, and contain vitamins A, B and C. They are well known for their laxative and digestive properties.

Purple Grapes are highly nutritious, containing natural sugars, potassium, iron and dietary fibre.
Raisins are dried grapes and offer relief from constipation, acidosis and anaemia.

Below: Beetroot

THE BEST IN BLUE

All these blue and purple foods are rich in minerals, boost cellular intake of oxygen and treat disorders of the blood, liver and immune system. They have excellent anti-cancer and anti-inflammatory and rejuvenating properties.

Blueberries
Red kidney beans
Dark plums
Aubergines (eggplants)
Beetroot (beet)
Cherries
Blue lentils
Garlic
Grapes
Figs
Blackberries
Bilberries
Aronia berries

Health benefits of blue & purple foods

The blue/purple pigment in fruits and vegetables contains anthocyanins which help to inhibit the cholesterol level in the blood. They are excellent antioxidants that play an important part in the diet, promote long term health and prevent age-related physical changes and chronic diseases. In addition they have anti-cancer and antibacterial properties, and are good for the health of the eyes, intestines, circulatory system and urinary tract.

Drinking the fresh juice of berry fruit, such as blueberries, cranberries and bilberries, may help prevent urinary tract infections. Such fruits are especially rich in vitamins A, B and C.

Blue and purple foods are rich in vitamin C, calcium, potassium, zinc, phosphorus and bioflavonoids. Many of these coloured foods are antioxidants. It is thought that they may lower the risk of certain cancers. Soft fruits are rich in pro-anthocyanins, which may improve immunity.

Below: Take advantage of the wide range of leafy salads available in any supermarket, and further enrich them with purple endive and juicy raisins.

Above: Purple striped aubergines

The Colour of Tranquillity

Choose foods from this group at times of the day when you need motivation and would like to relax with peace of mind, but avoid them when you are feeling – or want to feel – energetic.

Blue and purple foods will help maintain the flexibility of the blood vessels. Anthocyanin is a watersoluble pigment found in plants, more specifically in the cell vacuole. It is usually purple, blue or red and gives the colour of many flowers and plants. This pigment is also a powerful antioxidant and protects the plants from ultraviolet negative effects by absorbing the dangerous light rays.

Cutting the Risk of Cancer

Do remember that all blue and purple foods should be eaten as part of a healthy, balanced diet low in saturated fat and rich in a variety of fruits and vegetables. Over the last few years 30–40 per cent of all cancer deaths have been related to dietary factors, and these are potentially preventable with a simple change to diet and lifestyle.

Antioxidant properties of the natural colours or pigments fight against molecular oxidation by the free radicals. In our body an infinite number of chemical reactions take place every day. Chemical changes in the cells that use oxygen give birth to free radicals,

which can harm the cells and organs. An excessive amount of free radicals interact with parts of the other cells in the body and may even damage them. However, antioxidants in fruit, vegetables and plant foods counteract and neutralize these organic enemies. It is important to eat fruits and vegetables as they are rich in

Below: Red cabbage

Above: Raisins

antioxidants and phytochemical compounds, which can protect the cells and prevent serious diseases such as cancer and heart disorders.

Other Benefits

Mixed with the beneficial effects of vitamins A and C, anthocyanins are present in blue fruits and vegetables such as grapes, plums, red cabbage, red beetroot (beet), currants, figs and all kinds of berries. They are thought to improve visual accuracy, improve blood circulation to the nervous system and eyes and help to prevent eye disorders such as retinitis and myopia. Purple grapes have long been popular with convalescents recovering in hospital, and those seeking detoxification.

Blackcurrants are available nearly all the year round. They contain fibre, folic acid, flavonoids and are packed full of vitamin C. The bacteria-inhibiting anthocyanins found in the pigments can help prevent stomach upsets caused by E.coli. This antibacterial quality, combined with their anti-inflammatory properties, explains why blackcurrants sooth sore throats.

Above: Sharing a meal with a friend helps you feel better – and blue and purple foods will banish moody blues.

Aubergines (eggplants) help protect arteries from cholesterol damage by blocking the formation of free radicals.

Blue and purple plums are packed full of fibre, which is important for good bowel health.They are also high in vitamin E, which helps to prevent wrinkles as the body ages. Dried prunes and plums are even more concentrated than fresh fruit.

Left: Cherries
Below: Grapes

Left: Elderberries

Blue lagoon

Blueberries are not only an excellent source of betacarotene and vitamin C, they are also rich in flavonoids, which help to cleanse the system. Mixed with other dark purple fruits, such as blackberries and grapes, they make a highly nutritious and extremely delicious blend that can be stored in the refrigerator and relished throughout the day.

Makes 1 glass

90g/3½oz/scant 1 cup blackcurrants
   or blackberries
150g/5oz purple grapes
130g/4½oz/generous 1 cup blueberries
ice cubes

Cook's tip
This is a really tangy wake-up drink that you might find a bit too sharp. Add a dash of sugar or honey, or top up with mineral water to dilute it slightly, if you like.

1 Pull the blackcurrants or blackberries and grapes from their stalks.

2 Push the fruits through a juicer, saving a few for decoration. Place the ice in a medium glass and pour over the juice. Decorate with the remaining fruit and serve.

Energy 189kcal/805kJ; Protein 2.7g; Carbohydrate 47.2g, of which sugars 42g; Fat 0.1g, of which saturates 0g; Cholesterol 0mg; Calcium 74mg; Fibre 6.9g; Sodium 6mg.

Cool as a currant

Tiny, glossy blackcurrants are a virtual powerhouse of nutrients, packed with vitamins C and E, as well as essential iron, calcium and magnesium. Whizzed in a blender with plenty of crushed ice, they make a drink so deliciously thick and slushy that you might want to serve it with long spoons so that you can scoop up every last drop.

Makes 2 tall glasses

125g/4¼oz/generous 1 cup blackcurrants,
  plus extra to decorate
60ml/4 tbsp light muscovado (brown) sugar
good pinch of mixed (apple pie)
  spice (optional)
225g/8oz/2 cups crushed ice

1 Put the blackcurrants and sugar in a pan. (There is no need to string the blackcurrants first.) Add the mixed spice, if using, and pour in 100ml/3½fl oz/scant ½ cup water. Bring to the boil and cook for 2–3 minutes until the blackcurrants are completely soft.

2 Press the mixture through a sieve (strainer) into a bowl, pressing the pulp with the back of a wooden spoon to extract as much juice as possible. Leave to stand until completely cool.

Cook's tip
This is a great juice to make if you have plenty of blackcurrants in the freezer – they will thaw quickly in the pan. Redcurrants, or a mixture of redcurrants and blackcurrants, could also be used.

  Make a double quantity of this juice and store it in the refrigerator for up to a week – then it can be quickly blended with ice whenever you like.

3 Put the crushed ice in a blender or food processor with the cooled juice and blend for about 1 minute until slushy. Pour into glasses, decorate with blackcurrants and serve immediately.

Energy 136kcal/580kJ; Protein 0.7g; Carbohydrate 35.5g, of which sugars 35.5g; Fat 0g, of which saturates 0g; Cholesterol 0mg; Calcium 54mg; Fibre 2.3g; Sodium 4mg.

Aubergine soup with mozzarella and gremolata

Aubergines are low in calories and have a gentle natural laxative property that stimulates the liver and pancreas. They also have healing qualities and aid digestion. To enhance the flavour of the soup, a garlic-rich mixture is sprinkled on to it, which helps to lower the blood pressure and reduce cholesterol levels in the blood.

Serves 6

30ml/2 tbsp olive oil
2 shallots, chopped
2 garlic cloves, chopped
1kg/2¼lb aubergines (eggplants), trimmed
   and roughly chopped
1 litre/1¾ pints/4 cups chicken stock
150ml/¼ pint/⅔ cup double (heavy) cream
30ml/2 tbsp chopped fresh parsley
175g/6oz buffalo mozzarella, thinly sliced
salt and ground black pepper

For the gremolata

2 garlic cloves, finely chopped
rind of 2 lemons
15ml/1 tbsp chopped fresh parsley

1 Heat the oil in a large pan and add the shallots and garlic. Cook for 4–5 minutes, until soft. Add the aubergines and cook for 25 minutes, until soft.

2 Add the stock and cook for 5 minutes. Leave to cool, then purée in a food processor or blender until smooth. Return to the rinsed pan and season. Add the cream and parsley and bring to the boil.

Cook's tip
For a really fresh-tasting gremolata, add the lemon zest to the garlic and parsley at the last moment.

3 Mix the ingredients for the gremolata in a small bowl. Zest the lemon rind directly into the bowl.

4 Ladle the soup into bowls and lay the mozzarella on top. Scatter with gremolata and serve.

Energy 261kcal/1079kJ; Protein 7.5g; Carbohydrate 4.9g, of which sugars 4.3g; Fat 23.7g, of which saturates 13.1g; Cholesterol 51mg; Calcium 137mg; Fibre 3.5g; Sodium 124mg.

Braised red cabbage soup with beef and horseradish cream

Cabbage has been used for many years as a remedy for a variety of digestive and respiratory problems. It is rich in antioxidants, which can help strengthen and boost the immune system, helping the body overcome infection. It is packed full of vitamins, minerals and phytochemicals, which guard against bacterial and viral infection, heart disease and cancer.

Serves 6

900g/2lb red cabbage, hard core discarded
    and leaves shredded
2 onions, finely sliced
1 large cooking apple, peeled, cored
    and chopped
45ml/3 tbsp soft light brown sugar
2 garlic cloves, crushed
1.5ml/¼ tsp grated nutmeg
2.5ml/½ tsp caraway seeds
45ml/3 tbsp red wine vinegar
1 litre/1¾ pints/4 cups beef stock
675kg/1½lb sirloin joint, trimmed of fat
30ml/2 tbsp olive oil
salt and ground black pepper
watercress, to garnish

For the horseradish cream
15–30ml/1–2 tbsp fresh horseradish
10ml/2 tsp wine vinegar
2.5ml/½ tsp Dijon mustard
150ml/¼ pint/⅔ cup double (heavy) cream

1 Preheat the oven to 150°C/300°F/ Gas 2. Mix together the first eight ingredients and 45ml/3 tbsp of the stock. Season well, then put into a large buttered casserole and cover with a lid.

2 Bake for 2½ hours, checking every 30 minutes or so to ensure the cabbage is not becoming too dry. If necessary, add a few more tablespoons of the stock. Remove the casserole from the oven and set aside. Increase the oven temperature to 230°C/450°F/Gas 8.

3 Tie the sirloin with string. Heat the oil in a heavy frying pan until smoking. Add the beef and cook until browned all over.

4 Transfer to a roasting pan and roast for about 15–20 minutes for medium-rare or 25–30 minutes for well-done beef.

5 For the horseradish cream, grate the horseradish and mix with the wine vinegar, mustard and seasoning into 45ml/3 tbsp of the cream. Lightly whip the remaining cream and fold in the horseradish mixture. Chill until required.

6 Spoon the braised cabbage into a pan and pour in the remaining stock. Bring just to boiling point.

7 Remove the beef from the oven and leave to rest for 5 minutes, then remove the string and carve into slices.

8 Ladle the soup into bowls and divide the beef among them, resting on the cabbage. Spoon a little horseradish cream on to each serving of beef, and garnish with small bunches of watercress. Serve at once.

Energy 395kcal/1645kJ; Protein 29.4g; Carbohydrate 19.4g, of which sugars 18.5g; Fat 22.5g, of which saturates 11.1g; Cholesterol 92mg; Calcium 104mg; Fibre 3.8g; Sodium 97mg.

Sweet and sour red cabbage

The phytonutrients in such cruciferous vegetables as red and purple cabbage are thought to guard against prostate, colorectal and lung cancers. By increasing production of enzymes involved in detoxification, this brings about the cleansing process through which our bodies eliminate harmful compounds. Red cabbage is also a good source of vitamin C.

Serves 4–6

30ml/2 tbsp vegetable oil
½ large or 1 small red cabbage, cored
   and thinly sliced
1 large onion, chopped
50g/2 oz/1½ cups raisins or sultanas
   (golden raisins)
1 small apple, finely diced
15ml/1 tbsp sugar
120ml/4fl oz/½ cup dry red wine
juice of 1 lemon or 50ml/2fl oz/¼ cup
   lemon juice and cider vinegar
   mixed together
salt and ground black pepper

1 Heat the oil in a large pan, add the cabbage and onion and fry for 3–5 minutes, stirring, until the vegetables are well coated in the oil and the cabbage has softened slightly.

2 Add the raisins or sultanas, apple, sugar and wine to the pan and cook for 30 minutes, or until tender. Add more water or wine if the liquid has evaporated.

3 Towards the end of the cooking time, add the lemon juice, and vinegar if using, and season to taste. Serve hot or cold.

Cook's tip
This classic Jewish dish makes a great light and healthy lunch when served with rye bread.

Energy 148kcal/620kJ; Protein 2.2g; Carbohydrate 23.8g, of which sugars 22.2g; Fat 4g, of which saturates 0.4g; Cholesterol 0mg; Calcium 60mg; Fibre 2.9g; Sodium 19mg.

Duck with plum sauce

Plums are an excellent source of fibre, phosphorus and potassium. They also contain natural sugar for energy. Plums are thought to aid liver function and may help to lower cholesterol levels, especially valuable when eating this rich, fatty duck recipe. Serving this dish with steamed vegetables also gives more vitamins.

Serves 4

4 duck quarters
1 large red onion, finely chopped
500g/1¼lb ripe plums, stoned (pitted) and quartered
30ml/2 tbsp redcurrant jelly

1 Prick the duck skin all over with a fork to release the fat during cooking and help give a crisp result, then place the portions in a heavy frying pan, skin side down.

Cook's tip
Use very ripe plums in this dish, otherwise the mixture will be too dry and the sauce will be too sharp.

2 Cook the duck pieces for 10 minutes on each side, or until golden brown and cooked right through. Turn the duck from time to time, and ensure that the meat does not burn or scorch.

3 When the duck pieces are nicely golden brown, remove the pieces from the frying pan using a slotted spoon and keep warm.

4 Pour away all but 30ml/2 tbsp of the duck fat, then stir-fry the onion for 5 minutes, or until golden. Add the plums and cook for 5 minutes, stirring frequently. Add the jelly and mix well.

5 Replace the duck portions and cook for a further 5 minutes, or until thoroughly reheated. Season to taste before serving.

Energy 608kcal/2515kJ; Protein 15.1g; Carbohydrate 17.4g, of which sugars 17g; Fat 53.5g, of which saturates 14.5g; Cholesterol 0mg; Calcium 35mg; Fibre 2.2g; Sodium 102mg.

Stuffed aubergine with rice wine and ginger sauce

Aubergines should always be ripe when cooked otherwise they can be slightly toxic. These vegetables have laxative properties, calm the mind and stimulate the liver and pancreas. Ginger and garlic possess powerful anti-inflammatory properties, making this an ideal dish.

Serves 2

2 aubergines (eggplants)
1 egg
25ml/1½ tbsp vegetable oil
1 sheet dried seaweed
90g/3½oz/scant ½ cup minced (ground) beef
15ml/1 tbsp mirin or rice wine
15ml/1 tbsp dark soy sauce
1 garlic clove, crushed
5ml/1 tsp sesame oil
1 red chilli, seeded and shredded
1 green chilli, seeded and shredded
salt and ground black pepper
steamed rice, to serve

For the sauce
30ml/2 tbsp mirin or rice wine
30ml/2 tbsp dark soy sauce
5ml/1 tsp fresh root ginger, peeled and grated

1 Clean the aubergines and cut them into slices about 2.5cm/1in thick. Make two cross slits down the length of each slice, making sure not to cut all the way through. Sprinkle with a little salt and set aside.

2 Beat the egg and season with a pinch of salt. Coat a frying pan with 10ml/2 tsp oil and heat over medium heat.

3 Add the beaten egg to the frying pan and make a thin omelette, browning gently on each side.

4 Remove the omelette from the pan and cut it into thin strips. Cool the strips and then chill in the refrigerator.

5 Heat the remaining vegetable oil in a frying pan over high heat. Cut the seaweed into strips and stir-fry with the minced beef, mirin or rice wine, soy sauce and garlic. Once the beef is cooked through, drizzle with the sesame oil and set aside.

6 Place the shredded chillies in a bowl. Add the omelette strips and the cooked beef, and mix them together well. Rinse the salt from the aubergines and stuff each slice with a little of the beef and omelette mixture.

7 Place all the ingredients for the sauce into a frying pan, add 200ml/ 7fl oz/scant 1 cup of water and salt to taste, and heat over medium heat. Once the sauce is blended and bubbling, add the stuffed aubergine slices. Spoon the sauce over the aubergines and simmer for 15 minutes, or until the aubergines are soft and the skin has become shiny.

8 Transfer to a shallow dish and serve with steamed rice.

Energy 273kcal/1134kJ; Protein 14.3g; Carbohydrate 5.9g, of which sugars 5.3g; Fat 19.9g, of which saturates 5.2g; Cholesterol 122mg; Calcium 42mg; Fibre 4g; Sodium 1145mg.

Marinated baby aubergine with raisins and pine nuts

Baby aubergines are used in many dishes throughout the Mediterranean. They are thought to aid the function of the liver and the pancreas. The pine nuts may offer protection against heart disease and some cancers, and they can help ease digestive problems.

Serves 4

12 baby aubergines (eggplants),
    halved lengthways
200ml/7fl oz/scant 1 cup extra virgin olive oil
juice of 1 lemon
30ml/2 tbsp balsamic vinegar
3 cloves
40g/1½ oz/⅓ cup pine nuts
15g/½ oz/2 tbsp raisins
15g/½ oz/1 tbsp (white) sugar
1 bay leaf
large pinch of dried chilli flakes
salt and ground black pepper

1 Preheat the grill (broiler) to high. Place the aubergines, cut side up, in the grill pan and brush with a little of the olive oil. Grill (broil) for about 10 minutes, until slightly blackened, turning them over halfway through cooking.

2 To make the marinade, put the rest of the olive oil, the lemon juice, vinegar, cloves, pine nuts, raisins, sugar and bay leaf in a bowl. Add the chilli flakes and salt and pepper and mix well.

3 Place the hot aubergines in an earthenware or glass bowl and pour on the pine nut marinade. Allow to cool, turning the aubergines once or twice. Serve cold.

Cook's tip
If baby aubergines (eggplants) are unobtainable, cut larger aubergines into thick slices, remove the seeds, and proceed in the usual way.

Energy 207kcal/857kJ; Protein 1.1g; Carbohydrate 6.8g, of which sugars 6.7g; Fat 19.7g, of which saturates 2.6g; Cholesterol 0mg; Calcium 9mg; Fibre 1.2g; Sodium 4mg.

Beef and aubergine casserole

This delicious recipe uses lots of aubergines, which are rich in vitamins A, B and C, magnesium and phosphorus, which helps to prevent constipation. Tomatoes help to reduce problems in the digestive tract and bacteria in the bowel.

Serves 4

60ml/4 tbsp extra virgin olive oil
1kg/2¼lb good quality stewing steak
1 onion, chopped
2.5ml/½ tsp dried oregano
2 garlic cloves, chopped
175ml/6fl oz/¾ cup 1 glass white wine
400g/14oz can chopped tomatoes
2–3 aubergines (eggplants), total weight
    about 675g/1½lb
150ml/¼ pint/⅔ cup sunflower oil
45ml/3 tbsp finely chopped fresh parsley
salt and ground black pepper
toasted pitta bread, to serve

1 Cut the steak into four slices. Heat the oil in a large pan and brown the meat on both sides. As each piece browns, take it out and set it aside.

2 Add the chopped onion to the oil remaining in the pan and sauté it until translucent. Add the oregano and the garlic, then, as soon as the garlic becomes aromatic, return the meat to the pan and pour the wine over.

3 Allow the wine to bubble and evaporate for a few minutes, then add the tomatoes, with enough hot water to just cover the meat. Bring to the boil, lower the heat, cover and simmer for about 1 hour or a little longer, until the meat is tender.

4 Meanwhile, trim the aubergines and slice them into 2cm/¾in thick rounds, then slice each round in half.

5 Heat the sunflower oil and fry the aubergines briefly in batches over a high heat, turning them over as they become light golden. They do not have to cook at this stage and should not be allowed to burn. Lift them out and drain them on a platter lined with kitchen paper. When all the aubergines have been fried, season them.

6 When the meat feels tender, season it, then add the aubergines and shake the pan to distribute them evenly. From this point, do not stir the mixture as the aubergines will be quite fragile.

7 Add a little more hot water so that the aubergines are submerged in the sauce, cover the pan and simmer for 30 minutes more or until the meat is very tender. Sprinkle over the parsley and simmer for a few more minutes before serving with toasted pitta bread.

Cook's tip
This casserole is even better reheated the next day when the flavours and herbs have had time to develop and mingle.

Energy 565kcal/2364kJ; Protein 59.3g; Carbohydrate 8.6g, of which sugars 7.8g; Fat 29.9g, of which saturates 6.6g; Cholesterol 168mg; Calcium 67mg; Fibre 5.2g; Sodium 191mg.

Fresh figs baked with honey and vanilla

The chief benefits of fresh figs are that they serve as a natural laxative and are also slightly diuretic. They are rich in vitamins A, B and C, folic acid, calcium, copper, iron and zinc, which is thought to aid the digestive system, respiratory and immune system. Figs are good for pregnant women and for convalescing elderly people.

Serves 3–4

1 vanilla pod (bean)
30ml/2 tbsp caster (superfine) sugar
12 ripe figs
3–4 cinnamon sticks, broken into short pieces
45–60ml/3–4 tbsp clear honey
225g/8oz/1 cup chilled thick and creamy
  natural (plain) yogurt or clotted cream

1 To make the vanilla sugar, split a vanilla pod (bean) lengthways in half and scrape out the seeds using a pointed knife. Discard the pod and mix the seeds with the caster sugar.

2 Preheat the oven to 200°C/400°F/ Gas 6.

3 Wash the figs and pat them dry. Using a sharp knife, cut a deep cross from the top of each fig to the bottom, keeping the skin at the bottom intact. Fan each fig out in its quarters, so that it looks like a flower, then place them upright in a baking dish, preferably an earthenware one.

4 Sprinkle the vanilla sugar over each fig flower, tuck in the cinnamon sticks and drizzle with honey.

5 Bake for 15–20 minutes, until the sugar is slightly browned and caramelized but the honey and figs are still moist.

6 Spoon a dollop of yogurt or cream into the middle of each fig and scoop them up with your fingers, or serve the figs in bowls and let everyone help themselves to the yogurt or cream.

Variation
This recipe also works well with bananas. Split the unpeeled fruit down the middle and stuff with the vanilla sugar, cinnamon and honey.

Energy 198kcal/845kJ; Protein 2.3g; Carbohydrate 48.2g, of which sugars 48.2g; Fat 1g, of which saturates 0g; Cholesterol 0mg; Calcium 155mg; Fibre 4.5g; Sodium 39mg.

Blueberry pie

Blueberries are thought to have anti-cancer, anti-inflammatory and anti-bacterial properties, being good for the health of the eyes, intestines, circulatory system and urinary tract. They may inhibit free radicals, strengthen blood capillaries, and are useful in the treatment of rheumatoid arthritis as well as toning the cardiovascular system. They reduce the build-up of cholesterol.

Serves 6

2 × 225g/8oz ready-rolled shortcrust pastry
   sheets, thawed if frozen
800g/1¾lb/7 cups blueberries
75g/3oz/6 tbsp caster (superfine) sugar,
   plus extra for sprinkling
45ml/3 tbsp cornflour (cornstarch)
grated rind and juice of ½ orange
grated rind of ½ lemon
2.5ml/½ tsp ground cinnamon
15g/½oz/1 tbsp unsalted butter, diced
beaten egg, to glaze
natural (plain) yogurt, to serve

1 Preheat the oven to 200°C/400°F/
Gas 6. Use one sheet of pastry to line a
23cm/9in pie tin (pan), leaving the
excess pastry hanging over the edges.

2 Dampen the rim of the pastry case
with a little water.

3 Mix the blueberries, caster sugar,
cornflour, orange rind and juice, lemon
rind and cinnamon in a large bowl.
Spoon into the pastry case and dot
with the butter. Top the pie with the
remaining pastry sheet.

Variation
Blackcurrants or blackberries also
make an excellent filling for this pie.

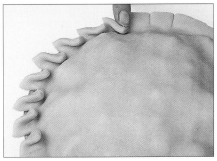

4 Trim off the excess pastry and cut out
decorations from the trimmings. Cut the
pastry edge at 2.5cm/1in intervals, then
fold each section over on itself to form
a triangle and create a sunflower edge.
Secure them to the pastry lid with a
little of the beaten egg.

5 Glaze the pastry with the egg
and sprinkle with caster sugar.
Bake for 30–35 minutes or until golden.
Serve warm or cold with yogurt.

Energy 371kcal/1559kJ; Protein 4.4g; Carbohydrate 55.8g, of which sugars 25.7g; Fat 16g, of which saturates 4.9g; Cholesterol 8mg; Calcium 93mg; Fibre 3.2g; Sodium 228mg.

Blackcurrant sorbet

Blackcurrants are rich in vitamins A, B, C and E, foliate, iron, manganese, antioxidants, fibre and natural sugar. They help with the absorption of iron, increase energy released from food and help the transportation of oxygen throughout the body. They aid liver function, speed up protein and fat metabolism and help in the healing of wounds.

2 Cover the pan and simmer for 5 minutes or until the fruit is soft. Cool slightly, then purée in a food processor or blender.

3 Set a large sieve (strainer) over a bowl, pour the purée into the sieve then press it through the mesh with the back of a spoon.

4 Pour the remaining measured water into the clean pan. Add the sugar and bring to the boil, stirring until the sugar has dissolved. Pour the syrup into a bowl. Cool, then chill. Mix the blackcurrant purée and sugar syrup together.

5 by hand: Spoon into a plastic tub or similar freezerproof container and freeze until mushy. Lightly whisk the egg white until just frothy. Spoon the sorbet into a food processor, process until smooth, then return it to the tub and stir in the egg white. Freeze for 4 hours or until firm.

using an ice cream maker: Churn until thick. Add the egg white and continue churning until it is firm enough to scoop.

6 Serve decorated with the blackcurrant sprigs.

Serves 6

500g/1¼lb/5 cups blackcurrants, trimmed
350ml/12fl oz/1½ cups water
150g/5oz/¾ cup caster (superfine) sugar
1 egg white
sprigs of blackcurrants, to decorate

Variation
Replace the blackcurrants with blackberries or blueberries.

1 Put the blackcurrants in a pan and add 150ml/¼ pint/⅔ cup of the measured water.

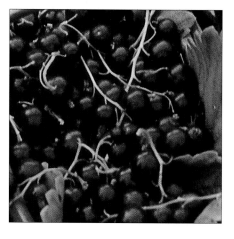

Energy 84kcal/361kJ; Protein 1.3g; Carbohydrate 21.2g, of which sugars 21.2g; Fat 0g, of which saturates 0g; Cholesterol 0mg; Calcium 58mg; Fibre 3g; Sodium 14mg.

Damson water ice

Damsons are a great source of calcium, iron, fibre and natural sugar. These little plums can help the body's system to maintain healthy bones and protect joints from gout and rheumatism. Damsons can also help to aid the digestive system from constipation and may prevent blood circulation problems.

Serves 6

500g/1¼lb ripe damsons, washed
450ml/¾ pint/scant 2 cups water
150g/5oz/⅔ cup caster (superfine) sugar
wafer biscuits, to serve

1 Put the damsons into a large pan and add 150ml/¼ pint/⅔ cup of the water. Cover the pan and simmer over a gentle heat for 10 minutes or until the damsons are tender.

2 Pour the remaining water into a second pan. Add the sugar and bring to the boil, stirring until the sugar has dissolved. Pour the syrup into a bowl, leave to cool, and chill in the refrigerator.

5 by hand: Pour the purée into a shallow plastic container. Stir in the syrup and freeze for 6 hours, beating once or twice to break up the ice crystals.

using an ice cream maker: Mix the purée with the syrup and churn until firm.

6 Spoon into tall glasses or dishes and serve with wafer biscuits.

3 Break up the cooked damsons in the pan with a wooden spoon and scoop out any free stones (pits).

4 Pour the cooked damsons and juices into a large sieve (strainer) set over a bowl. Press the fruit through the sieve and discard the skins and any remaining stones from the sieve.

Variation
Apricot water ice can be made in the same way. Flavour the water ice with a little lemon or orange rind or add a broken cinnamon stick to the pan when poaching the fruit.

Energy 130kcal/555kJ; Protein 0.6g; Carbohydrate 34.1g, of which sugars 34.1g; Fat 0g, of which saturates 0g; Cholesterol 0mg; Calcium 33mg; Fibre 1.5g; Sodium 3mg.

Index